SCHOLASTIC

Perfect Poems for
Teaching Vocabulary

Beth Sycamore

New York • Toronto • London • Auckland • Sydney
Mexico City • New Delhi • Hong Kong • Buenos Aires

Teaching Resources

To my daughter, Maddie, whose love of juicy words
never ceases to amaze me.

Edited by Joan Novelli
Cover design by Wendy Chan
Cover art by Shirley Beckes
Interior design by Holly Grundon
Interior illustrations by Dawn Apperly, Maxie Chambliss, Kate Flanagan, Mike Gordon, James Graham Hale, Amanda Haley, Anne Kennedy, Tammie Lyon, Maggie Smith, Bari Weissman

ISBN: 978-0-545-09439-9

Contents

About This Book

Music

I hear music

Rumbling trash cans

Hammers hammering

Books shutting, pencils tapping

Music—it's all around!

—Caitlin Mahar

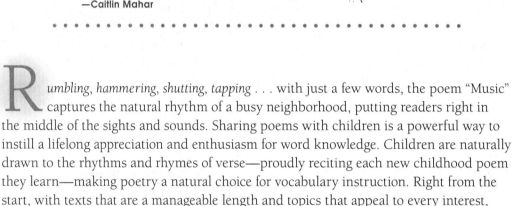

Rumbling, *hammering, shutting, tapping* . . . with just a few words, the poem "Music" captures the natural rhythm of a busy neighborhood, putting readers right in the middle of the sights and sounds. Sharing poems with children is a powerful way to instill a lifelong appreciation and enthusiasm for word knowledge. Children are naturally drawn to the rhythms and rhymes of verse—proudly reciting each new childhood poem they learn—making poetry a natural choice for vocabulary instruction. Right from the start, with texts that are a manageable length and topics that appeal to every interest, children fall in love with the lively language in poems and experience the pleasure of learning and using new words.

Perfect Poems for Teaching Vocabulary puts 50 poems at your fingertips, along with lessons that provide easy, research-based teaching routines for expanding children's repertoire of words. The poems are organized by 10 favorite early childhood themes to help you easily find poems that suit your instructional needs and children's interests. Each poem offers a playful context to teach a wealth of interesting words—from *spiffy* and *scrumptious* (pages 18 and 34) to *fearless* and *mighty* (pages 16 and 84). With lessons that target 50 words, and explorations that introduce many more, this book helps provide the language-rich learning experiences children need to develop a wide and robust vocabulary.

The lessons in this book were developed to support current research in vocabulary development, which touts the importance of repeated exposure to words and extended conversations (Roskos, Christie & Richgels, 2003; Beck, McKeown & Kucan, 2003; Beck, McKeown & Kucan, 2002; Beck & McKeown, 2001; Dickinson & Tabors, 2001). One of the best sources to advance children's vocabulary growth is children's literature (Roskos, Christie & Richgels, 2006; Nekovei & Ermis, 2006; Bennett-Armistead, Duke, & Moses, 2005; Beck, McKeown & Kucan, 2002). When children hear fiction and nonfiction read aloud, they are exposed to a myriad of interesting words. Repeated readings facilitate word learning when children are encouraged to be active participants. Tapping into children's background knowledge, posing child-friendly definitions, and orchestrating reflective discussions help keep children engaged in the read-aloud experience. Guided conversations using open-ended questions can prompt children to use new words as they share ideas and ask questions (Weitzman, 2002; Dickinson & Tabors, 2001). Follow-up activities are also critical to vocabulary development (Roskos, Christie & Richgels, 2006; Wasik, 2006). Through carefully planned learning experiences, children can practice using new words in a variety of ways. The poems and related activities in *Perfect Poems for Teaching Vocabulary* offer a lively context to spark an interest in words—which is a powerful catalyst for children's success as readers and writers.

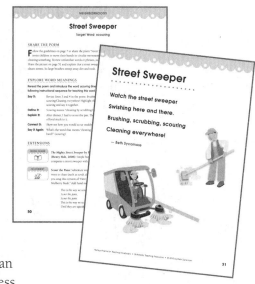

An Overview

The lessons in this book are designed for flexible use and are appropriate for both whole-group and small-group learning experiences. They're also structured to fit easily into your day. In just 10 minutes, and with very little prep work, you can share a poem and guide children through a scripted, sequential routine to teach a target word—from providing a definition to prompting children to make personal connections.

Whether you choose to use the lessons as part of your literacy block or as a "vocabulary break" at any time during the day, the poems and teaching routines provide a predictable format that will enhance children's awareness and understanding of words as they interact with a text, build comprehension, and have fun expanding word knowledge in an active way. An overview of the lesson format follows.

Reproducible Poem: Each lesson features a poem selected especially for its appeal to children and vocabulary-building potential. These poems appear on ready-to-use reproducible pages with illustrations that support the text. Photocopy these pages for small-group instruction or for children to share at home.

Share the Poem: A brief introduction to each poem provides prompts that promote conversation as you activate children's knowledge about and interest in the topic. For additional support for sharing and teaching with the poems, see Teaching With the Lessons (page 7).

Using Read-Alouds

Read-alouds are a great way to activate and build background knowledge. They also provide a context for children to hear and talk about the meanings of new words. Many of the lessons in this book feature read-aloud suggestions that extend the theme or topic and provide opportunities for children to apply target words in discussions. For example, after sharing the poem "Pizza Pizzazz" (page 40) and exploring the target word *sprinkle*, you can use *The Little Red Hen (Makes a Pizza)* by Philemon Sturges (Puffin 2002) to spark a discussion about toppings children like to sprinkle on a pizza (or other food). Additional titles for each theme appear in the Supplemental Book List (page 10).

Explore Word Meanings: The vocabulary lessons in *Perfect Poems for Teaching Vocabulary* are shaped by an instructional strategy developed by Isabel Beck and Margaret McKeown called "Text Talk" (Beck & McKeown, 2001). The Text Talk research and development project examined the benefits of vocabulary development in a read-aloud context. The authors' research with kindergarten and first-grade children captured the importance of children's trade books as a rich source for vocabulary instruction. These books are steeped in interesting and varied vocabulary. Young children might not be ready to read these delightful words on their own but they benefit from hearing and talking about them. Another important finding was the importance of effective teacher-student interactions to develop word meanings (Beck & McKeown, 2001). Engaging and focused discussions offer the perfect context to clarify or elaborate word meanings as well as make connections that are meaningful to young children. Beck and McKeown (2002) suggested a lesson framework to enhance children's awareness of words and their meanings as they interact with a text which includes contextualizing target words, using child-friendly definitions to explain target words, and encouraging children to relate the target words to personal experiences or interests. The lessons in this book tap into the power of the Text Talk approach to help you effectively expand children's repertoire of words.

Each lesson features a five-step, scripted routine for teaching a target word from the poem. These target words were selected both to intrigue young children and help shape a mature vocabulary. At the same time, the target words are easy enough to explain with everyday language. Based on the Test Talk framework, this routine includes the following sequence of steps to guide children in developing word knowledge:

Say It: Revisit the target word in the context of the poem.

Define It: Provide a brief, child-friendly definition of the word.

Explain It: Share a connection that personalizes the meaning of the word. Use the examples provided or create your own.

Connect It: Prompt children to make a connection with the target word and apply it to their own experiences.

Say It Again: Prompt children to say the word again with you.

Extensions: These engaging activities offer suggestions for connecting and extending learning in seven key areas: Art, Book Share, Dramatic Play, Math, Movement, Science, and Writing.

More Words to Explore: In addition to the target word for each lesson, you'll find several suggestions for teaching with other words from each poem. This section covers a range of words—from simple to complex. Some familiar words are used as springboards to explore figurative language, shades of meaning, synonyms, antonyms, homophones, and categories, such as *afraid* (page 16), *blanket* (page 26), *jars* (page 42), and *shout* (page 100). More abstract words were selected to enhance word-knowledge building, such as *pizzazz* (page 40), *bustling* (page 64), and *adore* (page 98). Use the instructional sequence for Explore Word Meanings as a model to help children learn these words.

Teaching With the Lessons

As you prepare to teach with the lessons in this book, review the following suggested procedures to maximize learning experiences.

1. Prepare   Copy the poem on chart paper or scan for use on an interactive whiteboard (for use with a large group). Make photocopies of the poem (for small-group instruction or for children to take home to share with friends and family). Read the poem in advance of the lesson to familiarize yourself with its rhythm and flow. Reading aloud helps! Review the scripted target-word routine (Explore Word Meanings) and make any desired changes—for example, you might substitute your own connection for Explain It.

2. Introduce the Poem   Follow the suggestions provided in each lesson (Share the Poem) to introduce the poem. Prompt children to share what they know about the topic—for example, when introducing "Fuzzy, Wuzzy Caterpillar" (page 68), you might ask: *Have you seen a real caterpillar or pictures of one? Tell me about it.*

3. Read the Poem Aloud   As you read the poem aloud, use intonation and phrasing to support the meaning of the text and the rhythm of the language. With a large group, use a pointer to track the print as you go. With small groups, have children follow along on individual copies of the poem.

4. Discuss the Poem   After sharing the poem, review any unfamiliar words or phrases. Provide prompts to invite children to share favorite parts and make personal connections to the poem. For example, after sharing "Maggy's Dog" (page 74), prompt children to make connections to their own experiences by asking: *What kinds of dogs do you see in your neighborhood? What do they look like?*

5. Explore Word Meanings   Use the instructional sequence to teach the target word. Allow time for children to have fun interacting with the word (Connect It). This might take the form of acting out the meaning—as with "Music" (page 48), for example: "Show me how you would hammer a short nail. Now show me how you would hammer a longer nail." Children may also interact with a word by making personal connections—for example, the lesson for "Carrots" (page 34) invites children to apply their understanding of the word *scrumptious*: "Tell me about a scrumptious snack you enjoy."

6. Extend the Lesson   Bring more meaning to the learning experience by planning deliberate opportunities for children to interact with each other and use the words they are learning. The Extensions section of each lesson provides suggestions for encouraging children to revisit the target word and apply it in different ways. For example, after sharing "Night Trucks" (page 54) and exploring the word *gaps* with children, you might take a walk together (around the school or neighborhood) to hunt for gaps, such as in playground equipment or fences. Documenting discoveries with children provides opportunities to use the target word in writing. Use the instructional sequence provided in each lesson (see step 5, above) as a model to teach with other words from each poem. (See also More Words to Explore, page 6.)

Tips for Expanding Word Knowledge

Consider the following suggestions to provide varied opportunities to explore meaning, extend children's thinking, and expand word knowledge.

Encourage Conversation
Intentional conversations facilitate and support children's vocabulary development. Good prompts can foster rich conversations with longer and more complex answers—for example, "What's another way to . . .?" and "Tell me how you . . .."

Promote Hands-On Experiences
Notice opportunities for children to act out the meaning of new words. For example, when you share "The Mail Carrier" (page 44), children can act out swinging the mailbag over their shoulder, then show how they can swing a bat.

Explore Relationships Among Words
Guide children to relate what they already know to new words. For example, in the poem "Crocodile" (page 72), how can they use what they know about the word *beads* to understand the meaning of *beady* ("beady eyes")?

Apply Words to Real Life
Have children think about how the words they are learning apply to their own lives. For example, as children listen to a poem about autumn leaves that *twirl* ("Autumn Leaves," page 92), they might visualize twirling spaghetti on a fork or twirling around themselves to understand the movement of leaves as they twirl to the ground.

Learn From Context
Model for children how to use context to uncover the meaning of new words. For example, after sharing the poem "Fearless" (page 16), revisit lines 1 and 2 ("I'm not afraid of anything!/I'm fearless; can't you see?") and think aloud about how you use the context of line 1 to understand the word *fearless* in line 2.

Identify Sensory Details
Explore how words can help us imagine the way something looks, smells, feels, tastes, or sounds. Does the word *gooey* ("How Many Ways to Say Cooking," page 36) help children picture how something they eat feels?

Investigate Ways Words Go Together
Sorting words, brainstorming word lists, labeling diagrams, and creating semantic word maps all encourage children to think more deeply about how words are related as they use word meanings to form categories. For example, the word *creeps* ("Fuzzy, Wuzzy Caterpillar," page 68) describes how a caterpillar moves. Children can suggest other words that describe how animals move, such as *gallop, hop, slither, climb,* and *flutter.*

Explore Synonyms, Antonyms, and Homophones
Broaden understanding by studying words with similar and opposite meanings, as well as words that sound the same (and may or may not be spelled the same). For example, *coast* ("On My Scooter," page 56) describes a way to move. You can also explore the meaning of the noun *coast* (*land that is at the edge of the ocean*).

Delight in Lively, Whimsical Language

Promote a love of language and inspire learning by taking time to simply enjoy the way words sound. For example, have fun with onomatopoeia (words that are names for sounds or words that sound like their meaning). *Fluttering* ("The Silent Snake," page 76), *pluck* ("Strawberries," page 88), and *chirping* ("Spring," page 98) are just a few examples children will encounter.

Connections to the Standards

Well-planned and purposeful learning experiences are important building blocks for early learning. The activities in *Perfect Poems for Teaching Vocabulary* are designed to support you in meeting learning recommendations and goals that correlate with the standards for language arts put forth by both Mid-continent Research for Education and Learning (McREL) and the Common Core State Standards Initiative. (For more information, see right.) Some of those standards include:

Vocabulary Acquisition and Use

- understands level-appropriate vocabulary, including synonyms, antonyms, homophones, and multiple-meaning words
- uses context clues, definition, restatement, compare/contrast to verify word meanings
- uses reading and context to understand the meaning of new words
- recognizes shades of meaning among similar words (such as *pull*, *tug*, *jerk*, and *tow*)
- groups words by categories (for example, *leap*, *glide*, *creep*, and *slide* all describe ways to move)
- makes connections among word meanings, personal experiences, and new situations
- applies words to real-life situations
- uses words acquired through read-alouds, discussions, and conversations

Listening and Speaking

- contributes to class and group discussions
- asks and responds to questions
- uses level-appropriate vocabulary in speech
- asks questions to clarify and deepen understanding
- expresses ideas clearly

A Final Note

The poems and activities suggested in this resource are just a starting point. Use the instructional framework and strategies with your own favorite poems, rhymes, and songs. Keep children's word learning experiences lively and fun! Let's give them something to talk about!

To Learn More

McREL, a nationally recognized nonprofit organization, has compiled and evaluated national and state standards—and proposed what teachers should provide for their students to grow proficient in language arts, among other curriculum areas. For more information, go to www.mcrel.org.

The Common Core State Standards Initiative is a state-led effort to establish a single set of clear educational standards aimed at providing students with a high-quality education. At the time that this book went to press, these standards were in the process of being finalized. To learn more, go to www.corestandards.org.

Supplemental Book List

As you teach with the lessons in this book, consider sharing additional read-alouds to activate and build background knowledge, as well as promote conversation and deepen understanding of related vocabulary.

All About Me

The Busy Body Book: A Kid's Guide to Fitness by Lizzy Rockwell (Crown Books for Young Readers, 2004)

Ella Sarah Gets Dressed by Margaret Chodos-Irvine (Harcourt, 2003)

Outside, Inside by Carolyn Crimi (Simon & Schuster, 1995)

The Squeaky Door by Margaret Read MacDonald (HarperCollins, 2006)

Truman's Loose Tooth by Kristine Wurm (Spirited Publishing, 2006)

Colors

Color Dance by Ann Jonas (Greenwillow, 1989)

Color (Eye Know) by Penelope Arlon (DK Publishing, 2007)

Red, Green, Blue: A First Book of Colors by Alison Jay (Dutton, 2010)

Red Sings From Treetops: A Year in Colors by Joyce Sidman (Houghton Mifflin, 2009)

Weaving the Rainbow by George Ella Lyon (Atheneum, 2004)

Food

How Did That Get to My Table? Pasta by Emily J. Dolbear (Cherry Lake Publishing, 2009)

Pancakes for Supper! by Anne Isaacs (Scholastic, 2006)

Tony and the Pizza Champions by Tony Gemignani (Chronicle, 2009)

Up, Down, and Around by Katherine Ayres (Candlewick, 2007)

Yummy! Eating Through a Day by Lee Bennett Hopkins (Simon & Schuster, 2000)

Neighborhoods

Big City Song by Debora Pearson (Holiday House, 2006)

Hammer Soup by Ingrid and Dieter Schubert (Front Street, 2004)

Hop! Plop! by Corey Rosen Schwartz & Tali Klein (Walker Books, 2006)

Playground Day! by Jennifer J. Merz (Clarion, 2007)

Supermarket by Kathleen Krull (Holiday House, 2001)

Transportation

Big, Bigger, and Biggest Trucks and Diggers (Chronicle, 2008)

Blades, Boards & Scooters (Popular Mechanics for Kids) by Keltie Thomas (Maple Tree Press, 2005)

Down in the Subway by Miriam Cohen (Star Bright Books, 2003)

I Wonder Why Planes Have Wings and Other Questions About Transportation by Christopher Maynard (Kingfisher, 2003)

Little Blue Truck by Alice Schertle (Harcourt, 2008)

Creepy, Crawly Critters

Butterfly House by Eve Bunting (Scholastic, 1999)

Clara Caterpillar by Pamela Duncan Edwards (HarperCollins, 2001)

Creepy, Crawly Baby Bugs by Sandra Markle (Walker Books for Young Readers, 2003)

Spiders by Nic Bishop (Scholastic, 2007)

Under One Rock: Bugs, Slugs, and Other Ughs by Anthony D. Fredericks (Dawn Publications, 2001)

Animals

Ackamarackus by Julius Lester (Scholastic, 2001)

Actual Size by Steve Jenkins (Houghton Mifflin, 2004)

An Egg Is Quiet by Dianna Aston (Chronicle Books, 2006)

Chicken, Chicken, Duck! by Nadia Krilanovich (Tricycle Press, 2011)

Dogs by Emily Gravett (Simon & Schuster, 2010)

Seeds & Plants

Flip, Float, Fly: Seeds on the Move by Joann Early Macken (Holiday House, 2008)

A Fruit Is a Suitcase for Seeds by Jean Richards (First Avenue Editions, 2006)

A Grand Old Tree by Mary Newell DePalma (Scholastic, 2005)

Muncha! Muncha! Muncha! by Candace Fleming (Simon & Schuster, 2002)

A Seed Is Sleepy by Dianna Hutts Aston (Chronicle Books, 2007)

Seasons

In November by Cynthia Rylant (Harcourt, 2000)

It's Spring! by Linda Glaser (Millbrook Press, 2002)

Listen, Listen by Phillis Gershator (Barefoot Books, 2007)

Sugarbush Spring by Marsha Wilson Chall (HarperCollins, 2000)

Summer: An Alphabet Acrostic by Steven Schnur (Clarion Books, 2001)

Earth & Sky

Cloud Dance by Thomas Locker (Harcourt, 2000)

Hottest, Coldest, Highest, Deepest by Steve Jenkins (Houghton Mifflin, 1998)

If You Find a Rock by Peggy Christian (Harcourt, 2000)

On Earth by G. Brian Karas (Puffin, 2008)

Stargazer's Alphabet: Night Sky Wonders From A to Z by John Farrell (Boyds Mills Press, 2007)

References & Resources

Beck, I. L. & McKeown, M. G. (1991). Conditions of vocabulary acquisition. In Barr, R., Kamil, M., Mosenthal, P., & Pearson, P. D. (Eds.) *Handbook of reading research* (Vol 2). New York: Longman.

Beck, I. L. & McKeown, M.G. (2001). Text talk: Capturing the benefits of read-aloud experiences for young children. *The Reading Teacher*, 55 (1): 10-20.

Beck, I. L., McKeown, M. G., & Kucan, L. (2002). *Bringing words to life: Robust vocabulary instruction*. New York: Guilford Press.

Beck, I. L., McKeown, M. G., & Kucan, L. (2003). Taking delight in words: Using oral language to build young children's vocabularies. *American Educator*, Spring, 36-46.

Bennett-Armistead, V. S., Duke, N. K. & Moses, A. M. (2005). *Literacy and the youngest learner: Best practices for educators of children from birth to 5*. New York: Scholastic.

Bergeron, B. S., Wermuth, S., Rhodes M. & Rudenga, E.A. (1996). Language development and thematic instruction: Supporting young learners at risk. *Childhood Education*, 72 (3): 141-145.

Biemiller, A. (2001). Teaching vocabulary: Early, direct, and sequential. *American Educator*, 25 (1): 24-28.

Biemiller, A. (2005). Vocabulary development and instruction: A prerequisite for school learning. In Neuman, S. B. and Dickinson, D. K. (Eds.) *The Handbook of Early Literacy Research* (Vol 2). New York: The Guilford Press.

Blachowicz, C. & Fisher, P. J. (2010). *Teaching vocabulary in all classrooms* (4th ed.). Columbus, OH: Allyn & Bacon.

Bodrova, E. and Leong, D. J. (2003). The importance of being playful. *Educational Leadership*, 60 (7): 50-53.

Bond, M. A. and Wasik, B. A. (2009). Conversation stations: Promoting language development in young children. *Early Childhood Education Journal*, 36 (6): 467-473.

Copple, C. & Bredekamp, S. eds. (2009) *Developmentally appropriate practice in early childhood programs: Serving children from birth through age 8*. Washington, DC: National Association for the Education of Young Children.

Dickinson, D. K. and Tabors, P. O. (2001). *Beginning literacy with language*. Baltimore, MD: Paul H. Brookes.

Dickinson, D. K. and Tabors, P. O. (2002). Fostering language and literacy in classrooms and homes. *Young Children*, 57 (2): 10-18.

Hargrave, A. C. and Senechal, M. (2000). A book-reading intervention with preschool children who have limited vocabularies: The benefits of regular reading and dialogic reading. *Early Childhood Research Quarterly*, 15 (1): 75-90.

Hart, B. and Risley, T. (2002). *Meaningful differences in the everyday experiences of young children*. Baltimore, MD: Paul H. Brookes.

Helm, J. H. and Beneke, S. (2003). *The power of projects: Meeting contemporary challenges in early childhood classrooms—strategies & solutions*. New York: Teacher's College Press.

Kindle, K. J. (2010). Vocabulary development during read-alouds: Examining the instructional sequence. *Literacy Teaching and Learning*, 14 (1 & 2): 65-88.

McGee, L. M. and Richgels, D. (2003). *Designing early literacy programs: Strategies for at-risk preschool and kindergarten children*. New York: The Gilford Press.

Mooney, C. G. (2005). *Use your words: How teacher talk helps children learn*. St. Paul: Redleaf Press.

Moore, P. and Lyon, A. (2005). *New essentials for teaching reading in pre-K–2*. New York: Scholastic.

Nekovei, D. L. and Ermis, S. A. (2006). Creating classrooms that promote rich vocabularies for at-risk learners. *Young Children*, 61 (6): 90-95.

Newman, S. B. (2006). Speak up! How to help build a rich vocabulary day by day. *Scholastic Early Childhood Today*, January/February: 12-13.

Roskos, K. A., Christie, J. F. & Richgels, D. J. (2003). The essentials of early literacy instruction. *Young Children*, 58 (2): 52-59.

Shedd, M. K. & Duke, N. K. (2008). The power of planning: Developing effective read-alouds. *Young Children*, 63 (6): 22-27.

Thompson, S. C. (2005). *Children as illustrators: Making meaning through art and language*. Washington, DC: National Association for the Education of Young Children.

Turner, T. and Krechevsky, M. (2003). Who are the teachers? Who are the learners? *Educational Leadership*, 60 (7): 40-43.

Wasik, B. A. (2006). Building vocabulary one word at a time. *Young Children*. 61 (6): 70–78.

Weitzman, E. & Greenberg, J. (2002). *Learning language and loving it: A guide to promoting children's social and language development in early childhood settings*. Toronto: The Hanen Program.

All By Myself

Target Word: fasten

SHARE THE POEM

Follow the guidelines on page 7 to share the poem "All By Myself." Discuss different ways children can take care of themselves. What are some things they can do all by themselves?

EXPLORE WORD MEANINGS

Reread the poem and introduce the word *fasten* (line 3). Use the following instructional sequence for teaching this word.

Say It: Revisit line 3: *I can comb my hair and fasten my shoe.* Highlight the word *fasten* and say it together.

Define It: *Fasten* means "to securely join one thing to another."

Explain It: Before I drive away in my car, I always fasten my seatbelt.

Connect It: Tell me how you fasten your shoes or sneakers. What is something else you fasten?

Say It Again: What's the word that means "to join one thing to another?" (*fasten*)

EXTENSIONS

BOOK SHARE

Safety First by Angela Royston (Heinemann, 2000): Draw attention to pictures of items that need to be fastened, such as seatbelts, straps on helmets, and life jackets.

MOVEMENT

Action Words: Model hand movements to demonstrate actions in the poem—for example, combing hair, fastening (tying) shoes, washing hands and faces, and putting away toys. Recite the poem with children, using the hand movements to act it out.

More Words to Explore

Use the instructional sequence (left) as a model for exploring other words in the poem, such as:

by **(line 2)**
Revisit the word *by*. Ask children if they know another word that sounds the same and means "to get something by paying money for it." (*buy*)

comb **(line 3)**
Display a comb. Ask: *What is something you do with comb? Can you think of something else you can use to detangle your hair?*

hands **(line 5)**
Recall words from the poem that name body parts (*hair, hands, face*). Write the words on chart paper and let children add others. Use the words to play a guessing game: *I'm thinking of something you use to clap. I'm thinking of something you can comb.*

All By Myself

These are things I can do,

All by myself.

I can comb my hair and fasten my shoe,

All by myself.

I can wash my hands and wash my face,

All by myself.

I can put my toys and blocks in place,

All by myself.

—Author Unknown

Before the Bath

Target Word: shines

SHARE THE POEM

Follow the guidelines on page 7 to share the poem "Before the Bath." Allow time for children to make personal connections between the poem and their own bathtime routines. Review unfamiliar words or phrases. For example, reread line 8 ("In just my skin"), then ask: *Can you really wear just your skin? What do you wear when you take a bath?*

EXPLORE WORD MEANINGS

Reread the poem and introduce the word *shines* (line 2). Use the following instructional sequence for teaching this word.

Say It:　　Revisit line 2: *And the water shines wet.* Highlight the word *shines* and say it together.

Define It:　If something shines, it looks bright and gives off light.

Explain It:　I always have a light on at night when I read. It shines on my book so that I can see all the words.

Connect It:　What is something that shines in the sky?

Say It Again:　What's the word to describe something that looks bright and gives off light? (*shines*)

EXTENSIONS

Flashlight Fun: Stock a science center with a few flashlights and assorted objects, such as coins, old CDs, pencils, pens, blocks, foil wrappers, small toys, rulers, and rubber bands. Have children direct the light on different objects. Which objects shine more than others?

Shiny Book: Have children look through old magazines for pictures of things that shine, such as headlights, a lighthouse, stars, and jewels. Have each child cut out a picture, glue it to a sheet of paper, and write or dictate a caption by completing the following sentence frame: *A/An _____ shines.* Put the pages together to make a class book.

More Words to Explore

Use the instructional sequence (left) as a model for exploring other words in the poem, such as:

wait (line 3)
Explain that the word *wait* means "to stay in place." Ask: *What is the word that sounds the same and refers to how heavy something or someone is?* (weight)

shivery-cold (line 7)
Encourage children to discuss how they feel when it's cold outside—for example, they might shiver or shake. Let children act out the word shivery-cold as you reread the poem.

warm (line 9)
Have children identify "temperature" words in the poem (*cold, colder, warm*). Use them to start a wall chart of weather words.

Before the Bath

It's cold, cold, cold,
And the water shines wet,
And the longer I wait,
The colder I get.

I can't quite make
Myself hop in,
All shivery-cold
In just my skin.

Yet the water's warm
In the tub, I know.
So—one, two, three,
And IN I go!

— Corinna Marsh

Fearless

Target Word: fearless

SHARE THE POEM

Follow the guidelines on page 7 to share the poem "Fearless." Briefly discuss things that might seem frightening to children. Invite volunteers to act out how they might look if they were scared or frightened. Review unfamiliar words or phrases.

EXPLORE WORD MEANINGS

Reread the poem and introduce the word *fearless* (line 2). Use the following instructional sequence for teaching this word.

Say It: Revisit lines 1 and 2 in the poem: *I'm not afraid of anything!/I'm fearless; can't you see?* Highlight the word *fearless* and say it together.

Define It: When you are fearless, you are not afraid of anything. You are brave.

Explain It: I'm fearless on a sled. When I sled down a hill, I'm not afraid to go fast.

Connect It: If you are fearless about bugs, what do you think you might say when you see one?

Say It Again: What's the word that means "not afraid of anything?" (*fearless*)

EXTENSIONS

DRAMATIC PLAY

Brave Behavior: Encourage children to explore being brave or fearless. Stock the dramatic play area with props related to familiar fears, such as the doctor's office (stethoscope and bandages), nighttime (teddy bears), and insects or snakes (plastic creepy crawlies). Let children use the props to act out being afraid and feeling brave.

WRITING

Fearless Me: Have children make four-page mini-books to show their fearless acts. On the first three pages help children complete and then illustrate the following sentence: *I am not afraid of _____ .* Add a final page: *I am fearless!*

More Words to Explore

Use the instructional sequence (left) as a model for exploring other words in the poem, such as:

afraid (**line 1**)
Explain that *afraid* and *fearless* have opposite meanings—they are antonyms. Invite children to take turns using both words.

frightened (**line 5**)
Explain that *frightened* means "afraid of someone or something." Ask questions such as: *Would you be frightened of a purring cat or a growling tiger?*

here (**line 7**)
Use the word *here* to show its meaning: *I keep extra tape here, in the drawer.* Ask: *What is the word for something your ears help you do?* (hear) Demonstrate by tapping a table or clapping. Ask: *What do you hear?* Point out that the words *here* and *hear* sound the same but have different spellings and meanings.

Fearless

I'm not afraid of anything!

I'm fearless; can't you see?

No snake or mouse or monster

can scare someone like me.

I'm not the least bit frightened!

All scary thoughts are gone . . .

(as long as I am here with you

and all the lights are on!).

—Kathleen M. Hollenbeck

Haircut

Target Word: spiffy

SHARE THE POEM

Follow the guidelines on page 7 to share the poem "Haircut." Discuss the poem, inviting children to share favorite parts or similar experiences. Review unfamiliar words or phrases. For example, some children may not be familiar with a barber. Explain that a barber is a person who cuts hair. If possible, share pictures of barber shops and chairs to build background knowledge.

EXPLORE WORD MEANINGS

Reread the poem and introduce the word *spiffy* (line 7). Use the following instructional sequence for teaching this word.

Say It: Revisit lines 7 and 8 in the poem: *And I look so spiffy special/When I get down from that chair.* Highlight the word *spiffy* and say it together.

Define It: *Spiffy* is another way to say that something looks really fine or stylish.

Explain It: My mother thought I looked very spiffy in my new dress.

Connect It: Tell me about a time you thought someone looked spiffy.

Say It Again: What's the word that means "something that looks really fine or stylish?" (*spiffy*)

EXTENSIONS

Spiffy Clips: Cut cardstock into 3-inch squares, triangles, or other shapes. Have children layer and glue bits of colorful paper, ribbon, and sequins on the cardstock. When dry, glue a clothespin to the back to make spiffy clips!

Word Substitutions: Let children suggest other words the poet might have considered for *spiffy*. Reread the poem, substituting their ideas—for example, "And I looked super fine." Which version do they like best? Why?

More Words to Explore

Use the instructional sequence (left) as a model for exploring other words in the poem, such as:

important (line 3)
Explain that if something is important, it has value or means a lot. Discuss important upcoming events and add them to the class calendar.

tickles (line 5)
Discuss why haircuts might tickle. Let children hunt for and share classroom items that tickle (such as feathers, fuzzy yarn, and paintbrushes).

cut (line 6)
Discuss things people cut, such as paper, grass, ribbon, and vegetables, as well as the tools they use. Ask questions such as: *Would I use a lawn mower or scissors to cut grass?*

Haircut

It's fun to get a haircut

And sit in the barber chair.

It makes me feel important

To sit so tall up there.

I think it sort of tickles

When they cut and comb my hair

And I look so spiffy special

When I get down from that chair!

—Mary Sullivan

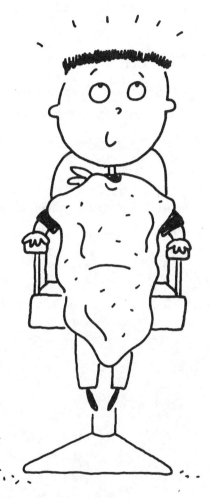

My Loose Tooth

Target Word: loose

SHARE THE POEM

Follow the guidelines on page 7 to share the poem "My Loose Tooth." Discuss the poem, inviting children to show how they would wiggle and jiggle a tooth. Review unfamiliar words or phrases. For example, reread line 12 ("and a hole in my head."). Ask: *What do you think happens when a tooth falls out? Do you really have a hole in your head?*

EXPLORE WORD MEANINGS

Reread the poem and introduce the word *loose* (line 1). Use the following instructional sequence for teaching this word.

Say It:	Revisit lines 1 and 2 in the poem: *I had a loose tooth,/ a wiggly, jiggly, loose tooth.* Highlight the word *loose* and say it together.
Define It:	When something is loose, it is not attached tightly.
Explain It:	When the seat on my bike is loose, I need to tighten it up before I go for a ride.
Connect It:	Tell me what happens if your sneaker laces are loose.
Say It Again:	What's the word that means "not attached tightly?" (*loose*)

EXTENSIONS

BOOK SHARE

Tooth on the Loose by Susan Middleton Elya (Putnam, 2008): A young girl has a loose tooth and is planning to use money from the tooth fairy to buy a birthday present for her father. If only her tooth would fall out in time!

WRITING

Oh No! Discuss problems that can arise when something is loose—for example, a loose button or leg on a chair. Help children complete and then illustrate the following sentence frame: *Oh no! My/ The _____ is loose!* Then have them share how they would solve the problem.

More Words to Explore

Use the instructional sequence (left) as a model for exploring other words in the poem, such as:

thread **(line 4)**
Explain that thread is like very thin string. Have children notice the way thread is used in clothing— for example, to stitch a pocket.

pulled **(line 5)**
Let children act out pulling different things—for example, a wagon. Brainstorm words with a similar meaning, such as *tug, jerk, tow,* and *drag.*

nickel **(line 11)**
Review the names for different coins. Ask questions to build understanding: *Which is worth more: a nickel or a penny? A dime or a nickel?*

My Loose Tooth

I had a loose tooth,
a wiggly, jiggly loose tooth.
I had a loose tooth,
hanging by a thread.

So I pulled my loose tooth,
this wiggly, jiggly loose tooth.
And put it 'neath the pillow
when I went up to bed.

The fairies took my loose tooth,
my wiggly, jiggly loose tooth.
So now I have a nickel
and a hole in my head.

—Ruth Kanarek

The Color Yellow

Target Word: crackling

SHARE THE POEM

Follow the guidelines on page 7 to share the poem "The Color Yellow." Invite children to recall interesting words the writer used to help them imagine the sounds of fireworks or the taste of popcorn. Review unfamiliar words or phrases. For example, share that a dandelion is a bright yellow wildflower.

EXPLORE WORD MEANINGS

Reread the poem and introduce the word *crackling* (line 2). Use the following instructional sequence for teaching this word.

Say It: Revisit lines 1 and 2 in the poem: *Yellow is big, booming, burning,/crackling fireworks.* Highlight the word *crackling* and say it together.

Define It: If something is crackling, it makes a short popping or snapping sound.

Explain It: The snow had a thin layer of ice on it. Each time I took a step, it made a crackling sound.

Connect It: Have you ever sat around a crackling fire? What sounds did the fire make?

Say It Again: What's the word that describes short popping or snapping sounds? (*crackling*)

EXTENSIONS

DRAMATIC PLAY

A Crackling Fire: Work with children to construct a "crackling" campfire. You might use blocks to form a ring and roll up newspaper and paint it brown to create logs. Add red, yellow, and orange cellophane "flames." Invite children to gather around to roast pretend marshmallows, tell stories, and stay warm.

WRITING

Crackle and Crunch: Invite children to say the word *crackling* with lots of expression. Brainstorm examples of onomatopoeia (such as *whoosh, whisper, roar*) and use the words to start a lively wall chart that children will love to read.

More Words to Explore

Use the instructional sequence (left) as a model for exploring other words in the poem, such as:

booming (line 1)
Model using a booming voice, then let children take turns doing the same. Discuss other words that describe how someone or something sounds.

fireworks (line 2)
Share pictures of fireworks and invite children to make connections to fireworks they've seen. Ask: *What other things light up the sky?*

tart (line 5)
Explain that if something is tart, it tastes sour. Ask: *If you wanted to taste something tart would you eat a lemon or a piece of chocolate?*

The Color Yellow

Yellow is big, booming, burning,

    crackling fireworks.

Yellow is the sound of popping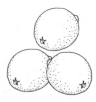

    buttery popcorn.

Yellow is the tart taste of lemons.

Yellow is bright, shocking

    lightning.

Yellow is a small dandelion in a big field.

—Brendan Nixon

Flower Boxes

Target Word: fragrant

SHARE THE POEM

Follow the guidelines on page 7 to share the poem "Flower Boxes." Invite children to talk about flowers they see in gardens, at grocery stores, or at farmers' markets. If possible, share pictures of the different flowers named in the poem. Review unfamiliar words or phrases. For example, *jonquils* (line 5) and *narcissus* (line 7) are other names for daffodils.

EXPLORE WORD MEANINGS

Reread the poem and introduce the word *fragrant* (line 4). Use the following instructional sequence for teaching this word.

Say It: Revisit lines 3 and 4 in the poem: *Are pretty flower boxes/Where fragrant blossoms grow.* Highlight the word *fragrant* and say it together.

Define It: *Fragrant* describes something that has a pleasant, sweet smell.

Explain It: In the morning my kitchen is fragrant with the cinnamon I add to my oatmeal.

Connect It: Would a kitchen be fragrant with a fresh apple pie or a bag of potatoes? Why?

Say It Again: What word means "a pleasant, sweet smell?" (*fragrant*)

EXTENSIONS

DRAMATIC PLAY

Flower Shop: Set up a flower shop that invites children to arrange fragrant bouquets and window boxes. Provide props such as tissue paper, pom-poms, pipe cleaners, cardboard boxes, and baskets. Model conversations that might occur in a flower shop.

SCIENCE

Sniff a Scent: Place samples of cinnamon, orange peel, cloves, dry cocoa, and other fragrant items in empty yogurt containers with lids. Poke holes in each lid. Make duplicates of each scent and mix them up. Have children smell the containers to make matching pairs.

More Words to Explore

Use the instructional sequence (left) as a model for exploring other words in the poem, such as:

ledges (line 2)
Explain that a ledge is a narrow shelf. Take a walk to look for ledges, such as a whiteboard ledge and a window ledge.

violets (line 6)
Display a picture of a violet. Revisit the poem to recall other names for flowers (*jonquils, narcissus, crocuses, tulips*). Let children label pictures of flowers for their flower shop.

crimson (line 8)
Share that crimson is a deep red color. Then explore other shades of red, such as scarlet, maroon, cherry red, and fire engine red. Let children create a display of classroom items (paper, books, blocks, and so on) to show different shades of red.

Flower Boxes

Outside apartment windows,
On ledges row on row,
Are pretty flower boxes
Where fragrant blossoms grow.

Yellow jonquils nodding,
Violets, purple blue,
White narcissus, crocuses,
Crimson tulips, too.

Perched on window ledges
Around our tall high-rise,
Lovely rainbow gardens,
Blooming in the skies.

— Jean Brabham McKinney

My Park

Target Word: steep

SHARE THE POEM

F ollow the guidelines on page 7 to share the poem "My Park." Invite children to describe favorite things they like to do at a playground or park. Discuss unfamiliar concepts or words, such as *footbridge* (line 2). Explain that a footbridge is a very narrow bridge that connects one place to another. It is made just for people to walk on.

EXPLORE WORD MEANINGS

Reread the poem and introduce the word *steep* (line 6). Use the following instructional sequence for teaching this word.

Say It: Revisit line 6 in the poem: *A slide made of silver with a very steep drop.* Highlight the word *steep* and say it together.

Define It: If something is steep, it goes up or down sharply.

Explain It: I ran out of breath when I climbed up the steep set of stairs.

Connect It: If a hill is steep, what would it look like? Show me with your hands.

Say It Again: What's the word for something that goes up or down sharply? (*steep*)

EXTENSIONS

MOVEMENT

We Are Climbing: Have children act out climbing a steep mountain as they sing "We are climbing a steep mountain, yes we are" to the tune of "She'll Be Coming 'Round the Mountain."

WRITING

Speech Bubble Stories: Work with children to paint a slide scene on mural paper. Have them draw pictures of themselves to add to the scene. Then give children precut speech bubbles and have them write or dictate a sentence about the steep slide—for example, "It's a little scary to go down the steep slide, but it's fun!" Add the speech bubbles to the scene.

More Words to Explore

Use the instructional sequence (left) as a model for exploring other words in the poem, such as:

blanket (line 1)
Let children tell what they know about blankets. Ask: *What are some things you can do with a blanket? How do you think a patch of grass is like a blanket?*

crawl (line 4)
Let children pretend to crawl through a tunnel. Ask: *What are other ways you can move on a playground?* Create a wall chart of movement words.

silver (line 6)
Where do children see the color silver in the classroom? They might, for example, find it on a computer, a faucet, and a clock. Based on their observations, have children describe this color. Guide them to incorporate words such as *shiny*, *metallic*, and *light gray*.

My Park

A blanket of green under my feet.

A footbridge of brown where the grass and pond meet.

A fountain of blue with a fish for a spout.

A tunnel of black to crawl in and out.

A rainbow of colors to climb up to the top.

A slide made of silver with a very steep drop.

— Beth Sycamore

A Rainbow of Colors

Target Word: fiery

SHARE THE POEM

Follow the guidelines on page 7 to share the poem "A Rainbow of Colors." Invite children to share stories about pets. Review unfamiliar words or phrases. For example, the color *fuchsia* may be new to children. If possible, share examples of this color, using familiar items such as a crayon or scarf.

EXPLORE WORD MEANINGS

Reread the poem and introduce the word *fiery* (line 7). Use the following instructional sequence for teaching this word.

Say It: Revisit line 7 in the poem: *A bright, fiery red fish—.* Highlight the word *fiery* and say it together.

Define It: If something is fiery, it is a bright red-orange color.

Explain It: Last night we watched the sun set over the mountains. It was a fiery red sunset.

Connect It: Tell me where you might see a truck that is fiery red.

Say It Again: What's the word that describes something that is bright red-orange? (*fiery*)

EXTENSIONS

Fiery Play Clay: Mix up a batch of fiery play clay. Combine four cups of flour, two cups of salt, and two tablespoons of ground cinnamon and ginger. Mix in two cups of water, two cups of vegetable oil, and red and orange food coloring to achieve a fiery tint. Knead until smooth. (Add more flour if the dough is sticky.) As children shape and mold the clay, discuss how the dough looks, feels, and smells. Store in an airtight container.

Picture Word Web: Have children cut out "fiery" pictures from magazines—sunsets, flowers, trucks, and so on. Write "Fiery Things" at the center of a web and have children arrange their pictures around it. Add labels and display.

More Words to Explore

Use the instructional sequence (left) as a model for exploring other words in the poem, such as:

peek (line 1)
Explain that *peek* means "to look secretly at someone or something." Say: *Show me how you would peek inside a package.*

see (line 2)
Compare the words *see* and *sea*. Guide children to notice that these words sound the same but have different spellings and meanings.

tangerine (line 5)
Explain that a tangerine is a type of fruit, but the word is also used to describe a reddish-orange color. Brainstorm other color words that also name fruits (such as *orange* and *lime*).

A Rainbow of Colors

I peek inside my fish bowl

And what do I see?

A rainbow of colors

Looking at me!

Tangerine and silver,

Fuchsia and sky blue,

A bright, fiery red fish—

And lemon-lime too!

— Beth Sycamore

Sidewalk Art

Target Word: squiggles

SHARE THE POEM

Follow the guidelines on page 7 to share the poem "Sidewalk Art." Review unfamiliar words or phrases. For example, share that a canvas (line 10) is a strong cloth stretched over a wooden frame that an artist uses to paint on.

EXPLORE WORD MEANINGS

Reread the poem and introduce the word *squiggles* (line 3). Use the following instructional sequence for teaching this word.

Say It: Revisit lines 1 through 5 in the poem: *Purple fingers,/ orange knees,/squiggles,/giggles,/green dust sneeze.* Highlight the word *squiggles* and say it together.

Define It: When someone draws squiggles, he or she is making short twisting lines.

Explain It: I drew a squiggle on a blank sheet of paper. Then I turned the squiggle into a flower.

Connect It: Use your finger to make a squiggle in the air.

Say It Again: What's the word that means "a short twisting line?" (*squiggle*)

EXTENSIONS

BOOK SHARE

The Squiggle by Carole Lexa Schaefer (**Dragonfly Books, 1999**): A young girl, on a walk with her class, spots a squiggle of string on the sidewalk. *Slither slish . . .* the squiggle becomes the tail of a scaly dragon, fireworks, the moon, and more.

WRITING

Wriggle Squiggle: Like the girl in *The Squiggle* (above), invite children to use their imagination to spot something in a squiggle. Give each child a piece of colorful string. Have children wriggle the string on their desk to form a squiggle. What can they transform their squiggle into? Have them glue the string to a sheet of paper, then write or dictate a sentence to share their imaginative thinking.

More Words to Explore

Use the instructional sequence (left) as a model for exploring other words in the poem, such as:

giggles (line 4)
Share examples of what might make someone *giggle*, such as a silly joke. Invite children to share jokes to bring out some giggles in the classroom.

pitter-patter (line 8)
Explain that *pitter-patter* describes light tapping sounds or beats. Draw children's attention to examples of this sound, such as rain on a window or quick, light footsteps in the hallway.

erases (line 9)
Write a sentence on a whiteboard. Ask: *What am I doing if I erase the sentence?* (making it disappear) Discuss times when children might choose to erase something.

Sidewalk Art

Purple fingers,
orange knees,
squiggles,
giggles,
green dust sneeze.
Drawing flowers,
drawing faces;
pitter-patter,
rain erases.
Concrete canvas,
clean and new;
you trace me,
then
I'll
trace
you.

— Jenny Whitehead

Beans, Beans, Beans

Target Word: few

SHARE THE POEM

Follow the guidelines on page 7 to share the poem "Beans, Beans, Beans." Invite children to tap their feet to the rhythm as you read this playful poem, then share their favorite type of bean. Review unfamiliar words or phrases—including names for different types of beans.

EXPLORE WORD MEANINGS

Reread the poem and introduce the word *few* (line 5). Use the following instructional sequence for teaching this word.

Say It: Revisit lines 4 and 5 in the poem: *Long, thin string beans—these are just a few.* Highlight the word *few* and say it together.

Define It: *Few* means "a small number of things or people."

Explain It: One night I went to a movie. I was very late and there were only a few seats left in the theater.

Connect It: What would you do if you had a lot of friends at your house and only a few cookies in your cookie jar?

Say It Again: What's the word that means "a small number of things or people?" (*few*)

EXTENSIONS

ART

Bean Mosaics: Stock the art center with different types of dried beans. Invite children to take a few of each and use them to create a design. Encourage children to use the word *few* as they describe the beans they used—for example, "I used a few small, dark-red beans and a few big, flat white beans."

MATH

1 2 3

Few and Many: Contrast the meaning of the words *few* and *many*. Play a question game to reinforce understanding. For example, ask: *Are there few or many windows in our room? Are there few or many papers on my desk?* Once children are familiar with the structure of the questions, let them take turns posing their own for classmates to answer.

More Words to Explore

Use the instructional sequence (left) as a model for exploring other words in the poem, such as:

long (line 4)
Review the difference between *long* and *short*. Let children hunt in pairs for objects in the classroom that represent both words.

thin (line 4)
Thin describes something that is not very wide. Hold up a thin marker and a thick one. Ask: *Which marker should I use if I want to draw thin lines?*

too (line 10)
Use the word *too* in a sentence: *I want some cookies, too!* Ask: *What word sounds the same, but means the number that comes after one?* (two) Review that *too* and *two* sound the same but have different spellings and meanings.

Beans, Beans, Beans

Baked beans,
Butter beans,
Big fat lima beans,
Long, thin string beans—
These are just a few.

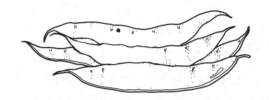

Green beans,
Black beans,
Big fat kidney beans,
Red hot chili beans,
Jumping beans, too.

Pea beans,
Pinto beans,
Don't forget shelly beans.
Last of all, best of all,
I like jelly beans.

—Lucia Hymes and James L. Hymes, Jr.

Carrots

Target Word: scrumptious

SHARE THE POEM

Follow the guidelines on page 7 to share the poem "Carrots." Allow time for children to make personal connections between the poem and vegetables they like to munch and crunch. Draw children's attention to words in the poem that describe how a carrot might sound when eaten.

EXPLORE WORD MEANINGS

Reread the poem and introduce the word *scrumptious* (line 2). Use the following instructional sequence for teaching this word.

Say It: Revisit lines 1 and 2 in the poem: *Carrots—/Scrumptious carrots.* Highlight the word *scrumptious* and say it together.

Define It: *Scrumptious* describes something that tastes delicious.

Explain It: Last night, I made a scrumptious cake. It tasted so good!

Connect It: Tell me about a scrumptious snack you enjoy.

Say It Again: What's the word that describes something that tastes delicious? (*scrumptious*)

EXTENSIONS

MATH
1 2 3

Let's Tally: Take a class survey: *What's your favorite treat?* List options and use tally marks to record children's responses. Count the tallies together to discover which scrumptious treat is the favorite.

WRITING

A Scrumptious Dessert: Discuss what makes a dessert scrumptious. Then work with children to make a large outline of a favorite dessert, such as an ice cream sundae. Have children roll paper, scrunch up paper, or tear paper to fill in the outline. Add a title to the mural: *A Scrumptious _____.*

More Words to Explore

Use the instructional sequence (left) as a model for exploring other words in the poem, such as:

carrots (line 1)
Use the word *carrots* as a springboard for creating a vegetable banner, complete with pictures and labels, that will inspire healthful eating habits.

lunch (line 3)
Review that lunch is a midday meal. What time does the class eat lunch? Discuss words that name other meals, such as *breakfast, supper,* and *dinner.*

munch (line 5)
Explain the meaning of the word—eating something in a continuous way (such as popcorn) that makes noise when you chew it. Let children name snacks they like to munch.

Carrots

Carrots—

Scrumptious carrots

All ready for lunch.

Take a bite.

Munch.

Munch.

Crunch!

— Beth Sycamore

How Many Ways to Say Cooking

Target Word: gooey

SHARE THE POEM

Follow the guidelines on page 7 to share the poem "How Many Ways to Say Cooking." Then invite children to share different things they do to help family members prepare meals. Review unfamiliar words or phrases. For example, reread line 9 ("taste the blast"). Explain that sometimes an explosion of flavor is called a *blast*.

EXPLORE WORD MEANINGS

Reread the poem and introduce the word *gooey* (line 1). Use the following instructional sequence for teaching this word.

Say It: Revisit lines 1 through 3 in the poem: *Smelly, yucky, gooey, chunky/easy baking, try making/fun tasting as you're baking.* Highlight the word *gooey* and say it together.

Define It: *Gooey* describes something that is soft and sticky.

Explain It: I took a bite of a hot slice of pizza. The cheese was so gooey, it dripped all over my chin.

Connect It: Tell me about something gooey you like to eat.

Say It Again: What's the word that describes something soft and sticky? (*gooey*)

EXTENSIONS

SCIENCE

A Gooey Experiment: Let children experiment with cornstarch and water to make a gooey substance. Have sponges and paper towels handy for cleanup.

WRITING

Gooey Grocery List: On chart paper, write a shopping list with children—gooey groceries only! Peanut butter and pudding are two possibilities. Illustrate the list, if possible, and have fun reading it aloud together.

More Words to Explore

Use the instructional sequence (left) as a model for exploring other words in the poem, such as:

chunky (line 1)
Share that something chunky has thick, solid pieces—like a chunky salsa or a chunky apple pie. Invite children to suggest other things that are chunky, such as a cookie with chunks of chocolate or a chunky vegetable soup.

baking (line 2)
Explain that baking is one way to cook food. Let children suggest words for other ways to cook, such as *frying*, *boiling*, and *toasting*.

yummy (line 5)
Explain that if something tastes good, you can say it's yummy. Reread the poem to find a word that means the opposite. (*yucky*, line 1)

How Many Ways to Say Cooking

Smelly, yucky, gooey, chunky,

easy baking, try making,

fun tasting as you're baking,

cookie, cookie, crunch, crunch

yummy, yummy, munch, munch

taste good, taste bad

if you have it you'll be glad

taste the fun

taste the blast

taste it while it lasts.

— Kiki Camerota

Mix a Pancake

Target Word: toss

SHARE THE POEM

Follow the guidelines on page 7 to share the poem "Mix a Pancake." Invite children to use hand movements to reinforce action words, such as *stir* and *mix*. Encourage children to share experiences they have had making pancakes or other foods with family members or friends.

EXPLORE WORD MEANINGS

Reread the poem and introduce the word *toss* (line 5). Use the following instructional sequence for teaching this word.

Say It: Revisit line 5 in the poem: *Toss a pancake.* Highlight the word *toss* and say it together.

Define It: *Toss* means "to throw something up in the air."

Explain It: When I make a pizza, I like to toss the pizza dough. I hold the dough in two hands and then toss it up in the air.

Connect It: Show me how you would toss a ball.

Say It Again: What's the word that means "to throw something up in the air?" (*toss*)

EXTENSIONS

DRAMATIC PLAY

Breakfast Café: Transform your dramatic play area into a breakfast café. Provide props (such as bowls, mixing spoons, and spatulas) that encourage children to stir, mix, and toss as they make pancakes and other breakfast foods.

WRITING

What Can We Toss? Brainstorm things people toss, such as a ball, a salad, and a coin. Help children complete and then illustrate the following sentence frame: *I can toss _____ .* Put their pages together with a cover, then staple to bind. Place the booklet in the class library for children to enjoy again and again.

More Words to Explore

Use the instructional sequence (left) as a model for exploring other words in the poem, such as:

stir (line 1)
Ask questions to provide practice with this word: *What would you use to stir some soup? What would you use to stir some mud?*

pancake (line 1)
Let children share what they know about pancakes, then work together to define this word—for example, "a thin, flat cake." Ask: *What two little words do you see in the word* pancake? Let children use the word *pancake* and other breakfast words to create a menu for their breakfast café.

mix (line 2)
Explain that *mix* means "to combine things." Ask: *What two colors would you mix to make orange? What snacks would you mix to make trail mix?*

Mix a Pancake

Stir a pancake,

Mix a pancake,

Pop it in a pan.

Cook a pancake,

Toss a pancake,

Catch it if you can!

— Christina Rossetti

Pizza Pizzazz

Target Word: *sprinkle*

SHARE THE POEM

Follow the guidelines on page 7 to share the poem "Pizza Pizzazz." Discuss toppings children like to put on their pizzas. Review unfamiliar concepts or words. For example, share that mozzarella is a type of cheese that is often used to make pizza.

EXPLORE WORD MEANINGS

Reread the poem and introduce the word *sprinkle* (line 5). Use the following instructional sequence for teaching this word.

Say It: Revisit line 5 in the poem: *Top it all off with a sprinkle of spice.* Highlight the word *sprinkle* and say it together.

Define It: A sprinkle is something you scatter in small bits.

Explain It: Sometimes I order ice cream with chocolate sprinkles.

Connect It: Tell me what you might sprinkle on oatmeal or a cupcake.

Say It Again: What's the word for something that you scatter in small bits? (*sprinkle*)

EXTENSIONS

BOOK SHARE

The Little Red Hen (Makes a Pizza) by Philemon Sturges (Puffin, 2002): In this familiar folktale with a twist, Little Red Hen gathers ingredients to make a pizza. As a followup, invite children to share toppings they like to sprinkle on a pizza.

WRITING

Sprinkle Poem: As a class, create a list poem about the word *sprinkle*. Start by writing "We can sprinkle…" then have children suggest ideas—cheese on spaghetti, water on plants, raisins on cereal, and so on.

More Words to Explore

Use the instructional sequence (left) as a model for exploring other words in the poem, such as:

pizzazz (title)
Explain that *pizzazz* means "stylish," "amazing," or "exciting." Let children take turns using the word to describe someone or something.

delicious (line 1)
Brainstorm words with a similar meaning, such as *tasty, yummy,* and *scrumptious.* (See "Carrots," page 34 for a related lesson.)

slice (line 6)
Share that a slice is a thin piece of something cut from a larger piece. Let children take turns naming foods that come in slices, such as bread, cheese, and cake.

Pizza Pizzazz

Have you ever seen a more delicious sight

than a pizza dressed up to go out at night?

Thick tomato sauce and mozzarella cheese,

mushrooms, sausage, more peppers, please!

Top it all off with a sprinkle of spice.

It's looking so good—Hey, who took a slice?

— Liza Charlesworth

The Corner Store

Target Word: squishy

SHARE THE POEM

Follow the guidelines on page 7 to share the poem "The Corner Store." Invite children to make personal connections between details in the poem and their own experiences in a corner store or market. Discuss shapes and sizes of different containers and how items are displayed to help shoppers find what they are looking for.

EXPLORE WORD MEANINGS

Reread the poem and introduce the word *squishy* (line 6). Use the following instructional sequence for teaching this word.

Say It: Revisit line 6 in the poem: *Bags of squishy bread.* Highlight the word *squishy* and say it together.

Define It: *Squishy* describes something that is soft.

Explain It: At night I like to sleep on a squishy pillow. It is so soft my head sinks right in.

Connect It: Do you have something squishy that you take to bed? Tell me about it.

Say It Again: What's the word that describes something that is soft? (*squishy*)

EXTENSIONS

DRAMATIC PLAY

At the Corner Store: Transform the dramatic play area into a corner store with empty, clean containers representing items on a corner-store shelf. Offer a tub of play clay for making food to add to the offerings, such as squishy rolls. Encourage sign-making for daily specials.

WRITING

Squishy Sentences: Brainstorm squishy things, such as rolls, pillows, and marshmallows. Help children complete and then illustrate the following sentence frame: *A _____ is squishy.* Create a display of "squishy sentences" to promote conversations that include this word.

More Words to Explore

Use the instructional sequence (left) as a model for exploring other words in the poem, such as:

jars **(line 2)**
Brainstorm foods packaged in jars, such as jam, pickles, and peanut butter. Discuss uses for other containers, such as bags, boxes, and cans.

sticky **(line 2)**
Discuss things that are sticky, such as gum and glue. Ask: *Would you want to wash your hands after handling something sticky? Why?*

crusty **(line 7)**
Let children imagine eating crusty bread. Does it crunch when they take a bite? Ask: *When you step on crusty snow, how does it sound?*

The Corner Store

What's inside the corner store?

Jars of sticky jam—

Cherry, peach, and grape.

Boxes of crackers—

Oodles of every shape.

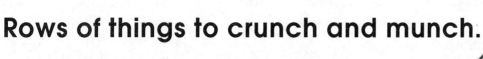

Bags of squishy bread—

Wheat and crusty white.

Rows of things to crunch and munch.

What a scrumptious sight!

— Beth Sycamore

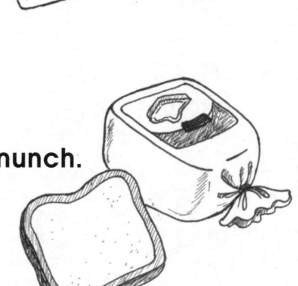

The Mail Carrier

Target Word: bundled

SHARE THE POEM

Follow the guidelines on page 7 to share the poem "The Mail Carrier." Discuss how mail is delivered to school and other places in the neighborhood. Review unfamiliar words or phrases, such as *mail carrier*. Explain that a mail carrier delivers mail to people in a neighborhood, often carrying the mail in bags or carts.

EXPLORE WORD MEANINGS

Reread the poem and introduce the word *bundled* (line 4). Use the following instructional sequence for teaching this word.

Say It: Revisit lines 3 and 4 in the poem: *And messages from around the world/Are bundled up inside.* Highlight the word *bundled* and say it together.

Define It: *Bundle* means "to tie or roll up a number of things together."

Explain It: Sometimes I bundle old magazines with string. This is how I keep the magazines together.

Connect It: What is something you might want to bundle?

Say It Again: What's the word that means "to tie or roll up a number of things together?" (*bundle*)

EXTENSIONS

DRAMATIC PLAY

Sort and Bundle: Stock the dramatic play area with twine, scissors, empty bags, and all sorts of junk mail. Invite children to sort and bundle the mail, then place it in a bag to deliver.

SCIENCE

We Recycle! Discuss with children the benefits of recycling—for example, to reduce the amount of trash we produce. As an environmental science project that also instills a civic spirit, work with children to bundle newspapers and other papers at school for recycling. Children can keep track of the bundles they recycle to see what a difference they make!

More Words to Explore

Use the instructional sequence (left) as a model for exploring other words in the poem, such as:

whistling (line 1)
Explain that *whistling* means "making a high pitch sound." Have fun whistling together!

swings (line 1)
Let children pantomime the meaning of this word—for example, walking with a swing in their step, swinging a bat, and swinging a bag over their shoulder.

messages (line 3)
Discuss words the poet might have used in place of *messages* (such as *letters*). Ask: *What kinds of things do people send in the mail?*

The Mail Carrier

The whistling mail carrier swings along.

    Her bag is deep and wide,

And messages from around the world

    Are bundled up inside.

The mail carrier's walking up our street.

    Soon she'll ring our bell.

Perhaps there'll be a letter stamped

    In Asia. Who can tell?

— Author Unknown

Monkey Bars

Target Word: hoist

SHARE THE POEM

Follow the guidelines on page 7 to share the poem "Monkey Bars." As you read, invite children to pantomime the actions. Allow time for children to share favorite playground activities.

EXPLORE WORD MEANINGS

Reread the poem and introduce the word *hoist* (line 8). Use the following instructional sequence for teaching this word.

Say It: Revisit line 8 in the poem: *I can hoist myself up.* Highlight the word *hoist* and say it together.

Define It: *Hoist* means "to lift something heavy."

Explain It: This morning I saw a crane hoisting huge steel beams at a construction site.

Connect It: Show me how you would hoist something heavy.

Say It Again: What's the word that means "to lift something heavy?" (*hoist*)

EXTENSIONS

BOOK SHARE

***What Is a Pulley?* (Welcome Books) by Lloyd G. Douglas (Scholastic, 2002):** Full-color photographs and simple text introduce young readers to the science behind the pulleys that hoist flags and other things. Prompt children to use the word *hoist* as they explore and discuss the way these simple machines work.

SCIENCE

Hoist It! Tie a long piece of rope to a plastic pail and gather objects of different weights that will fit in the pail. Use the rope to hang the pail from a tree limb (or other suitable place). Let children take turns hoisting different objects (one at a time) in the pail. Discuss which were easier/harder to hoist.

More Words to Explore

Use the instructional sequence (left) as a model for exploring other words in the poem, such as:

monkey bars (line 1)
Display pictures of different types of monkey bars. Invite children to tell how they think this piece of playground equipment got its name.

dangle (line 6)
Invite children to think about sitting on a swing. Ask: *Do your feet touch the ground?* Explain that if their feet don't touch the ground, they *dangle*. Have children suggest other places their feet might dangle, such as when they're sitting on the bus or on their bed.

sway (line 7)
Explain that *sway* means "to move from side to side." Have children pretend they are branches on a tree, swaying in the breeze.

Monkey Bars

I like monkey bars.

I can swing like a monkey.
I can hang upside down.
I can climb to the top.
I can jump to the ground.

I can dangle my feet.
I can sway with one hand.
I can hoist myself up.
I can shout when I land.

Hey! Look at me!

— Beth Sycamore

Music

Target Word: hammering

SHARE THE POEM

Follow the guidelines on page 7 to share the poem "Music." As you read, invite children to pantomime actions, such as "hammers hammering," "books shutting," and "pencils tapping." Ask: *How do you think these sounds are like music?*

EXPLORE WORD MEANINGS

Reread the poem and introduce the word *hammering* (line 3). Use the following instructional sequence for teaching this word.

Say It: Revisit line 3 in the poem: *hammers hammering.* Highlight the word *hammering* and say it together.

Define It: *Hammering* means "hitting or pounding something."

Explain It: I had to hammer a nail in the wall to hang up a picture.

Connect It: Show me how you would hammer a short nail. Now show me how you would hammer a longer nail.

Say It Again: What's the word that means "hitting or pounding something?" (*hammering*)

EXTENSIONS

DRAMATIC PLAY

Carpenters at Work: Stock the dramatic play area with pounding benches, small (plastic) hammers, foam blocks, golf tees (for nails), and safety glasses. Encourage discussion as children work. Ask: *Why do you need to be careful when you use a hammer? Why do you think a carpenter might wear safety glasses?*

MOVEMENT

Hammering: Invite children to "hammer" along as you substitute their names in this version of "Johnny Works With One Hammer."

> *[Child's name] hammers one nail, one nail, one nail*
> *[Child's name] hammers one nail*
> *Now there are two.*
> *[Repeat with new names and the numbers three, four, and so on.]*

More Words to Explore

Use the instructional sequence (left) as a model for exploring other words in the poem, such as:

rumbling (line 2)
Discuss the meaning of this word (*deep, rolling sounds*), then talk about things that rumble, such as a heavy truck, a train coming down the tracks, and a hungry tummy.

shutting (line 4)
Invite children to pantomime examples of this word—for example, shutting a window, shutting a door, and shutting down a computer.

tapping (line 4)
Demonstrate the meaning of this word by inviting children to take turns tapping out a rhythm on their desk with a pencil. Discuss other ways people tap rhythms, such as with drumsticks and their feet.

Music

I hear music

rumbling trash cans

hammers hammering

books shutting, pencils tapping

music—it's all around!

— Caitlin Mahar

Street Sweeper

Target Word: scouring

SHARE THE POEM

Follow the guidelines on page 7 to share the poem "Street Sweeper." As you read, invite children to move their hands in circular movements to pretend they are cleaning something. Review unfamiliar words or phrases, such as *street sweeper.* Share the picture on page 51 and explain that a street sweeper is a vehicle that cleans streets. Its large brushes sweep away dirt and trash.

EXPLORE WORD MEANINGS

Reread the poem and introduce the word *scouring* (line 3). Use the following instructional sequence for teaching this word.

Say It: Revisit lines 3 and 4 in the poem: *Brushing, scrubbing, scouring/Cleaning everywhere!* Highlight the word *scouring* and say it together.

Define It: *Scouring* means "cleaning by scrubbing hard."

Explain It: After dinner, I had to scour the pan. There was a lot of food stuck to it.

Connect It: Show me how you would scour muddy shoes.

Say It Again: What's the word that means "cleaning by scrubbing hard?" (*scouring*)

EXTENSIONS

BOOK SHARE

The Mighty Street Sweeper by Patrick Moore (Henry Holt, 2006): Simple but informative text compares a street sweeper with other work vehicles.

MOVEMENT

Scour the Pans: Substitute words that describe ways to clean (such as *scrub, dust,* and *polish*) as you sing this version of "Here We Go Round the Mulberry Bush." Add hand movements!

> *This is the way we scour the pans,*
> *Scour the pans,*
> *Scour the pans.*
> *This is the way we scour the pans,*
> *Until they are squeaky clean.*

More Words to Explore

Use the instructional sequence (left) as a model for exploring other words in the poem, such as:

watch (line 1)
Discuss words with similar meanings, such as *look, see, glance,* or *stare.* Create a word wall to promote an awareness of these words and their meanings.

swishing (line 2)
Revisit the illustration on page 51 and point out the scrubbers that "swish" back and forth. Have fun saying the word *swishing* together. Point out that some words sound like what they describe. Share other examples, such as *roar, tick tock,* and *buzz.*

brushing (line 3)
Have children show how they brush their teeth. How would they brush a dog?

Street Sweeper

Watch the street sweeper

Swishing here and there.

Brushing, scrubbing, scouring

Cleaning everywhere!

— Beth Sycamore

City Bus

Target Word: scoot

SHARE THE POEM

Follow the guidelines on page 7 to share the poem "City Bus." Allow time for children to make personal connections between the poem and their own experiences on a city or school bus. Review unfamiliar words or phrases. For example, reread line 2 ("Put in your fare—"). Explain that a fare is money people pay to ride a bus, train, taxi, or subway.

EXPLORE WORD MEANINGS

Reread the poem and introduce the word *scoot* (line 7). Use the following instructional sequence for teaching this word.

Say It: Revisit lines 7 and 8 in the poem: *Let's scoot downtown;/ We have friends to meet.* Highlight the word *scoot* and say it together.

Define It: *Scoot* means "to go somewhere in a hurry."

Explain It: Sometimes I need to scoot to the grocery store to pick up something for dinner.

Connect It: Tell me why you might scoot over to a neighbor's house.

Say It Again: What's the word that means "to go somewhere in a hurry?" (*scoot*)

EXTENSIONS

BOOK SHARE

Bus Route to Boston by Maryann Cocca-Leffler (Boyds Mills Press, 2000): Two young sisters and their mom hop on a bus and scoot downtown.

WRITING

Where Are You Going? Brainstorm places children "scoot," such as to the bus stop in the morning or the playground after lunch. Help children complete and then illustrate the following sentence frame: *At _____ [time of day], I scoot to _____ [place].*

More Words to Explore

Use the instructional sequence (left) as a model for exploring other words in the poem, such as:

bus (line 1)
Discuss how a bus is different from other modes of transportation. Create an illustrated transportation word web.

fare (line 2)
Review the meaning of *fare*. Place coins in the dramatic play area for children to act out paying the fare to ride a bus, train, taxi, or subway.

meet (line 8)
Review the meaning of *meet*. Ask: *What word sounds the same but is something people eat?* (meat) Review that these words sound the same but have different spellings and meanings.

City Bus

Hop on the bus.

Put in your fare—

A seat by the window

To go anywhere!

Hop on the bus.

Hop in your seat—

Let's scoot downtown;

We have friends to meet.

— Beth Sycamore

Night Trucks

Target Word: gaps

SHARE THE POEM

Follow the guidelines on page 7 to share the poem "Night Trucks." Discuss the poem, inviting children to describe what is happening. Review unfamiliar words or phrases. For example, revisit lines 3 and 4 ("They flay at the night with/Their paddles of sound."). Help children understand that the trucks are breaking up the darkness and quiet of the night with their headlights and loud engine noise.

EXPLORE WORD MEANINGS

Reread the poem and introduce the word *gaps* (line 7). Use the following instructional sequence for teaching this word.

Say It: Revisit line 7 in the poem: *They sew up the gaps*. Highlight the word *gaps* and say it together.

Define It: A gap is a space between things.

Explain It: When I look in the mirror, I see a gap between my two front teeth.

Connect It: Tell me why a farmer might want to fill in a gap in a fence.

Say It Again: What word describes a space between things? (*gap*)

EXTENSIONS

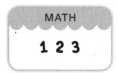

Fill the Gaps: Work with children to build a connected row of blocks, using different shapes and sizes. Remove several blocks to create gaps. Let children take turns filling a gap with the missing block, sharing the name for the shape as they do so.

Neighborhood Gaps: Take a walk around the school to look for gaps, such as in fences, playground equipment, sidewalks, and walls. If possible, document children's discoveries with photos. Use the word *gap* in a caption for each photo.

More Words to Explore

Use the instructional sequence (left) as a model for exploring other words in the poem, such as:

roar (line 5)
When a truck roars, it makes a loud sound. Brainstorm other things that roar, such as a lion or a crowd at a baseball game.

brake (line 6)
After teaching the word *brake*, introduce the word *break*. Let children take turns using each word. Review that these words sound the same but have different spellings and meanings.

distances (line 8)
Share the meaning of the word *distance*: how far apart two people, places, or things are. Invite children to talk about "far distances" they have traveled—for example, to visit a relative.

Night Trucks

They tunnel through darkness,

    Their eyes on the ground.

They flay at the night with

    Their paddles of sound.

They roar and they rumble.

    They screech and they brake.

They sew up the gaps

    That far distances make.

—Thelma Ireland

On My Scooter

Target Word: coast

SHARE THE POEM

Follow the guidelines on page 7 to share the poem "On My Scooter." Discuss the poem, inviting children to act out riding a scooter. Review unfamiliar words or phrases. For example, reread line 6 ("With my feet planted perfectly still."). Explain that when people plant their feet it means they place each foot firmly in one spot.

EXPLORE WORD MEANINGS

Reread the poem and introduce the word *coast* (line 5). Use the following instructional sequence for teaching this word.

Say It: Revisit lines 3 through 5 in the poem: *One GIGANTIC push down the hill/First I rock/And then I coast.* Highlight the word *coast* and say it together.

Define It: *Coast* means "to move forward without effort."

Explain It: Sometimes when I ride my bike, I stop pedaling and see how far I coast.

Connect It: Tell me what it feels like to coast on a bike or scooter.

Say It Again: What's the word that means "to move forward without effort?" (*coast*)

EXTENSIONS

BOOK SHARE

Six Hogs on a Scooter **by Eileen Spinelli (Orchard, 2000):** Follow six pigs as they try all sorts of ways to get to the opera on time—even hopping on a scooter!

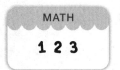
MATH

1 2 3

Coasting Cars: Give children toy cars. Use tape to mark a starting line. How far can the cars coast? Have children make predictions, then take turns giving their cars a push to find out. Encourage use of the word *coast* as children compare predictions to results.

More Words to Explore

Use the instructional sequence (left) as a model for exploring other words in the poem, such as:

gigantic (**line 3**)
Create a "size-word" wall chart. Have children illustrate each word with pictures they cut from magazines.

rock (**line 4**)
Invite children to sit on the floor, wrap their arms around their knees, and rock back and forth. Work together to define the word as used in this way, then discuss another meaning of the word (*a stone*).

still (**line 6**)
Explain that *still* means "not moving or making a sound." Let children point out times during the day when they are still—such as when listening to a story.

On My Scooter

One foot on,

One foot off,

One GIGANTIC push down the hill.

First I rock.

And then I coast,

With my feet planted perfectly still.

— Beth Sycamore

That One's Me!

Target Word: glide

SHARE THE POEM

Follow the guidelines on page 7 to share the poem "That One's Me!" Invite children to describe what is happening. Review unfamiliar words or phrases. For example, reread lines 3 and 4 ("Have you seen a jet/go screaming by?"). Ask: *Is the jet really screaming? What do you think is happening?*

EXPLORE WORD MEANINGS

Reread the poem and introduce the word *glide* (line 6). Use the following instructional sequence for teaching this word.

Say It: Revisit lines 5 and 6 in the poem: *Have you seen a submarine/glide beneath the sea?* Highlight the word *glide* and say it together.

Define It: *Glide* means "to move smoothly and quietly."

Explain It: When I go skating at the rink, I glide across the ice.

Connect It: Tell me why it would be difficult to glide on a dirt road.

Say It Again: What's the word that means "to move smoothly and quietly?" (*glide*)

EXTENSIONS

BOOK SHARE

Night Gliders by Joanne Ryder (Troll Communications, 1997): This enchanting nature book captures a flurry of activity as four flying squirrels glide from tree to tree.

SCIENCE

Fold and Fly: Help children make simple paper airplanes. In an open area, let them take turns tossing the planes in the air. Encourage children to describe how each plane glides. Then have them experiment with different ways to toss the planes. Discuss how this affects how the planes glide, how far they glide, and so on.

More Words to Explore

Use the instructional sequence (left) as a model for exploring other words in the poem, such as:

helicopter (line 1)
Recall words in the poem that name vehicles (*helicopter, jet, submarine, bicycle*). Discuss how the vehicles are alike and different.

hover (line 2)
Create a picture display of birds and insects that hover, such as hummingbirds and bees. Encourage use of the word *hover* in related conversations.

beneath (line 6)
Invite children to act out the meaning of *beneath* as they use it in a sentence—for example, placing their feet beneath the desk or hanging one painting beneath another on the wall.

That One's Me!

Have you seen a helicopter

hover in the sky?

Have you seen a jet

go screaming by?

Have you seen a submarine

glide beneath the sea?

Have you seen a bicycle?

That one's me!

—Tony Mitton

Underground Rumbling

Target Word: tumbling

SHARE THE POEM

Follow the guidelines on page 7 to share the poem "Underground Rumbling." Invite children to recall words the writer used to help the reader imagine what a subway train sounds like. Share that subway trains go very fast. They travel through tunnels deep under the ground to carry people in cities from one stop to another.

EXPLORE WORD MEANINGS

Reread the poem and introduce the word *tumbling* (line 7). Use the following instructional sequence for teaching this word.

Say It: Revisit lines 7 and 8 in the poem: *Seems to come tumbling/Out of the ground.* Highlight the word *tumbling* and say it together.

Define It: If something tumbles, it rolls and tosses about.

Explain It: I dropped my bag this morning, and it went tumbling down the stairs.

Connect It: Would you want to tumble on a soft mat or hard floor? Tell me why.

Say It Again: What's the word that describes something that rolls and tosses about? (*tumbling*)

EXTENSIONS

BOOK SHARE

Subway Ride by Heather Lynn Miller (Charlesbridge, 2009): Simple rhythmic text captures the sights and sounds of a city subway ride.

MOVEMENT

Tumbling Down: Gather children on a mat to sing a version of "Jack and Jill" that features their names. Substitute two children's names as you repeat the verse and let those children act out the words to reinforce the meaning of "tumble."

More Words to Explore

Use the instructional sequence (left) as a model for exploring other words in the poem, such as:

street (line 2)
Use this word as a springboard for exploring names for different kinds of roads. Ask questions to stretch understanding—for example, *How is a street different from a highway?*

shivering (line 3)
Invite children to demonstrate how they might shiver if it's cold.

hollow (line 5)
Share another use of the word *hollow*, as with tubes. Let children suggest things that are hollow, such as a straw. (Revisit the word *hollow* with the poem "Sunflowers," page 90.)

Underground Rumbling

At times when we're walking
Along the street,
There comes a shivering
Under our feet.

And a hollow, roaring,
Rumbling sound
Seems to come tumbling
Out of the ground.

We've heard it again
And again and again.
So, of course, we know
It's the subway train.

—James S. Tippett

Beetles in the Garden

Target Word: iridescent

SHARE THE POEM

Follow the guidelines on page 7 to share the poem "Beetles in the Garden." Discuss the poem, inviting children to recall interesting words the writer used to help them picture what beetles look like. Build background knowledge by sharing that a beetle is an insect with hard, shiny wings. A ladybug is a beetle. So is a firefly.

EXPLORE WORD MEANINGS

Reread the poem and introduce the word *iridescent* (line 7). Use the following instructional sequence for teaching this word.

Say It: Revisit lines 7 through 9 in the poem: *iridescent/red or/ yellow.* Highlight the word *iridescent* and say it together.

Define It: If something is *iridescent,* it looks shiny, with rainbow-like colors.

Explain It: I gave my daughter a T-shirt with iridescent sequins on it. She likes the way all the colors shimmer and shine.

Connect It: Describe what you would see on an iridescent seashell.

Say It Again: What's the word that means "shiny with rainbow-like colors?" (*iridescent*)

EXTENSIONS

ART

Beetles That Shine: Let children create illustrations to go with the poem, using iridescent paints (or glitter glue) to make their beetles shine! Copy the poem on chart paper and display with children's art.

BOOK SHARE

Beetles and Bugs: A Touch and Feel Adventure **by A. Wood (Silver Dolphin Books, 2003):** Simple, descriptive text paired with detailed illustrations invites readers into the colorful world of beetles and bugs.

More Words to Explore

Use the instructional sequence (left) as a model for exploring other words in the poem, such as:

large (line 3)
Challenge children to find a word in the poem that means the opposite of *large* (*small*).

flat (line 5)
Discuss the meaning of the word, then let children hunt for objects in the room that are flat, using words or pictures to document their findings.

humpy (line 6)
Discuss what the author means by "humpy tall." Ask: *What animal has one or two humps?* (camel)

Beetles in the Garden

Beetles

may be

large or small,

shaped from

flat to

humpy tall,

iridescent,

red or

yellow—

every one

is a hungry fellow.

— Elsie S. Lindgren

Busy Bee

Target Word: balance

SHARE THE POEM

Follow the guidelines on page 7 to share the poem "Busy Bee." Discuss the poem, inviting children to make sounds and use hand motions to show how a busy bee might move. Review unfamiliar words or phrases. For example, reread line 4 ("bathed in summer sun"). Ask: *What do you think the bee might be doing? How is this like taking a bath?*

EXPLORE WORD MEANINGS

Reread the poem and introduce the word *balance* (line 3). Use the following instructional sequence for teaching this word.

Say It: Revisit line 3 in the poem: *Balance on a buttercup.* Highlight the word *balance* and say it together.

Define It: *Balance* means "to keep something from falling over."

Explain It: Adam and Kai were careful to balance the blocks when they built their tower.

Connect It: Show me how you can balance on one foot.

Say It Again: What's the word that means "to keep from falling over?" (*balance*)

EXTENSIONS

BOOK SHARE

Mirette on the High Wire **by Emily Arnold McCully (Putnam, 1997):** This Caldecott Medal winner tells the story of a high-wire master and a young girl who sets out to learn the art, first by balancing on a clothesline strung across the backyard.

WRITING

Balance at Work: Display pictures that capture people using balance—for example, a dancer balancing on one foot or a waiter balancing plates. Have children write or dictate sentences to go with them.

More Words to Explore

Use the instructional sequence (left) as a model for exploring other words in the poem, such as:

bustling (line 2)
Share that *bustling* means "to move around in a busy way." Gather children in an open space and let them bustle about.

itty-bitty (line 5)
Share words with a similar meaning, such as *tiny, small,* and *teeny.* Create a fun display of itty-bitty things.

bold (line 6)
Discuss the meaning of the word *bold* (brave, willing to try something new), then let children share ways they are bold—for example, when trying an unusual food.

Busy Bee

Buzz among the blossoms,

bustling, busy one.

Balance on a buttercup,

bathed in summer sun.

Itty-bitty bumble,

bold and brave, a bee;

how can one so tiny

scare big kids like me?

— Kathleen M. Hollenbeck

Firefly

Target Word: damp

SHARE THE POEM

Follow the guidelines on page 7 to share the poem "Firefly." Discuss the poem, inviting children to describe what is happening. Review unfamiliar words or phrases. For example, reread line 3 ("And slowly lights his lamp"), then ask: *Is the firefly really lighting a lamp? What do you think he is doing? How is this like turning on a lamp?*

EXPLORE WORD MEANINGS

Reread the poem and introduce the word *damp* (line 1). Use the following instructional sequence for teaching this word.

Say It: Revisit line 1 in the poem: *Although the night is damp.* Highlight the word *damp* and say it together.

Define It: When something is *damp,* it is a little bit wet.

Explain It: When I am finished with breakfast, I wipe the table with a damp rag.

Connect It: Tell me how your clothes might get damp.

Say It Again: What's the word that means "a little bit wet?" (*damp*)

EXTENSIONS

ART

Sponge Art: Let children experiment with damp sponges to make paintings. Begin by reviewing the difference between "dry," "damp," and "wet." Model using a damp sponge to cover a sheet of paper with one or more colors. Show how you can blend colors with a damp sponge and use it to blot paint and create textures.

DRAMATIC PLAY

Housekeeping Helpers: Discuss things people use to clean up, such as sponges and rags. Stock the dramatic play area with a selection of these items. Demonstrate how to make a rag damp by getting it wet and wringing it out. Discuss situations children can role-play using a damp rag, such as wiping the table after snack or cleaning up a spill on the floor.

More Words to Explore

Use the instructional sequence (left) as a model for exploring other words in the poem, such as:

ventures (line 2)
The firefly ventures out at night, even though it might be wet/rainy. Ask children: *Would you venture outside in a storm?* Have them explain why or why not.

slowly (line 3)
Lead children in moving slowly from one place to another. Ask: *What are some times you move slowly?* (for example, when they wake up)

lamp (line 3)
Discuss differences between lamps and other kinds of lights, such as chandeliers, flashlights, and street lights.

Firefly

Although the night is damp,

The little firefly ventures out,

And slowly lights his lamp.

— Author Unknown

Fuzzy, Wuzzy Caterpillar

Target Word: creeps

SHARE THE POEM

Follow the guidelines on page 7 to share the poem "Fuzzy, Wuzzy Caterpillar." Discuss the poem, inviting children to describe what is happening. (Consider sharing a book about the life cycle of a caterpillar to build background knowledge as needed. See Book Share, below.) Review unfamiliar words or phrases—for example, line 3 ("He spins himself a blanket"). Ask: *Is the caterpillar really making a blanket? What do you think he is spinning? How is this like a blanket?*

EXPLORE WORD MEANINGS

Reread the poem and introduce the word *creeps* (line 2). Use the following instructional sequence for teaching this word.

Say It: Revisit line 2 in the poem: *In the garden creeps.* Highlight the word *creeps* and say it together.

Define It: *Creeps* means "to move very slowly and quietly."

Explain It: Sometimes my cat creeps down the stairs at night. I can't hear him at all.

Connect It: Tell me why you might creep somewhere. *(for example, at home if the baby is taking a nap)*

Say It Again: What's the word that means "to walk very slowly and quietly?" *(creeps)*

EXTENSIONS

BOOK SHARE

***Face to Face With Caterpillars* by Darlyne Murawski (National Geographic Children's Books, 2009):** Fascinating photographs and informative text bring a photographer's field experiences to life to teach about metamorphosis and more.

WRITING

What's in Your Garden? Help children complete and then illustrate the following sentence frame: *A/an _____ creeps in the garden.* Display the sentences to create a "garden" display that children can read.

More Words to Explore

Use the instructional sequence (left) as a model for exploring other words in the poem, such as:

fuzzy **(line 1)**
Invite children to name fuzzy things. Work with children to create a display they can explore.

spins **(line 3)**
Discuss other uses of this word—for example, a top spins; a tire swing at a playground spins; children might spin or twirl around.

fast **(line 4)**
Point out that in the poem *fast* does not mean "moving quickly." Share that "fast asleep" means "in a deep sleep." Revisit lines 3 and 4 of the poem. Ask: *What do you think is happening?*

Fuzzy, Wuzzy Caterpillar

Fuzzy, wuzzy caterpillar
In the garden creeps.
He spins himself a blanket
And soon falls fast asleep.

Fuzzy, wuzzy caterpillar
Wakes up by and by
To find he has wings of beauty,
Changed to a butterfly.

— Author Unknown

Tiny World

Target Word: creek

SHARE THE POEM

Follow the guidelines on page 7 to share the poem "Tiny World." Discuss the poem, inviting children to recall an interesting detail about each insect. Review unfamiliar words or phrases. For example, reread line 3 ("Ladybug dressed in a spotted shell"). Ask: *Do you think a ladybug can get dressed like you? What is the spotted shell the ladybug puts on?*

EXPLORE WORD MEANINGS

Reread the poem and introduce the word *creek* (line 6). Use the following instructional sequence for teaching this word.

Say It: Revisit line 6 in the poem: *Dragonfly buzzing over the creek.* Highlight the word *creek* and say it together.

Define It: A *creek* is similar to a stream or brook; it is smaller than a river.

Explain It: I like to wade in the creek behind my grandma's house.

Connect It: If you went for a hike and came across a creek, tell me what you would see.

Say It Again: What's the word for something that is like a stream or brook and is smaller than a river? (*creek*)

EXTENSIONS

BOOK SHARE

Abe Lincoln Crosses a Creek: A Tall, Thin, Tale **by Deborah Hopkinson (Random House Books for Young Readers, 2008):** Join in on the adventure as Abe and his good friend Austin decide to cross the rain-swollen waters of Knob Creek on a log.

SCIENCE

The World of Water: Review words that name bodies of water: *creek, stream, puddle, pond, river, lake, ocean,* and so on. Discuss how they are alike and different, then work with children to create a "picture-dictionary" display of selected words. Let each child choose a body of water to illustrate. Have children write or dictate a definition, then combine their work to create a colorful, informative display.

More Words to Explore

Use the instructional sequence (left) as a model for exploring other words in the poem, such as:

spotted (line 3)
Work with children to create a display featuring pictures of animals with spotted patterns, such as ladybugs, cheetahs, cows, snakes, fish, and giraffes. Encourage use of the word *spotted* in children's conversations about the animals.

wiggly (line 5)
Discuss the meaning of *wiggly*, then let children act out holding a wiggly worm or a wiggly puppy.

buzzing (line 6)
Let children act out "buzzing" like dragonflies over a creek, making a low, continuous hum as they move about. To explore another form of this word (*buzz*), see "Busy Bee" (page 64).

Tiny World

Tiny beetle, busy and black

Spider creeping across a crack

Ladybug dressed in a spotted shell

Grasshopper green, you hide so well

Wiggly worm in a robin's beak

Dragonfly buzzing over the creek

All so tiny, all so small—

To you, I must seem very TALL!

— Mary Sullivan

Perfect Poems for Teaching Vocabulary • Scholastic Teaching Resources • © 2010 by Beth Sycamore

Crocodile

Target Word: beady

SHARE THE POEM

Follow the guidelines on page 7 to share the poem "Crocodile." Invite children to pantomime the majestic walk of the crocodile. Discuss words that are fun to read out loud, such as *rumpy* and *bumpy*. Share that the American Crocodile is a large reptile that can grow up to 15 feet long. (Measure this length with children to provide a visual.) Crocodiles live on water and on land.

EXPLORE WORD MEANINGS

Reread the poem and introduce the word *beady* (line 1). Use the following instructional sequence for teaching this word.

Say It: Revisit line 1 in the poem: *Crocodile: beady eyes.* Highlight the word *beady* and say it together.

Define It: If an animal has beady eyes, its eyes are small, round, and shiny.

Explain It: I saw a cat last night with bright-green beady eyes.

Connect It: Do you have a stuffed animal with beady eyes? Tell me about it.

Say It Again: What's the word that describes eyes that are small, round, and shiny? (*beady*)

EXTENSIONS

ART

Connect With Collage: Display pictures of animals with beady eyes, such as crocodiles, birds, and fish. Provide assorted collage materials, such as magazine pages, wallpaper samples, scrap paper, bits of fabric, foil wrappers, sequins, and cellophane. Let children choose a beady-eyed animal and create a collage, using shiny materials to make eyes that are beady and bright.

BOOK SHARE

Crocodiles and Alligators by Seymour Simon (HarperCollins, 2001): Full-color photographs capture the unique features of crocodiles and alligators.

More Words to Explore

Use the instructional sequence (left) as a model for exploring other words in the poem, such as:

bumpy (line 3)
Display pictures of crocodiles and point out the bumpy skin. Have children share examples of other bumpy things, such as a bike tire, sneaker treads, and a rubber door mat.

dragging (line 4)
Invite children to pantomime dragging something heavy and then something light.

majestic (line 5):
Share the meaning of this word and discuss words with a similar meaning, such as *impressive* and *grand*. Invite children to act out the word as they take a majestic walk to lunch, recess, and so on.

Crocodile

Crocodile: beady eyes

So beady and bright.

Back rumpy and bumpy.

Long tail dragging behind.

Such a majestic walk you have,

Sinking in on your prey.

— Katie Touff

Maggy's Dog

Target Word: shaggy

SHARE THE POEM

Follow the guidelines on page 7 to share the poem "Maggy's Dog." Invite children to share their own experiences with dogs. Review unfamiliar words or phrases. For example, discuss the word *grim*, and invite children to make a grim expression. Then have them tell if they think the dog in the poem is frightening or not, and how they know.

EXPLORE WORD MEANINGS

Reread the poem and introduce the word *shaggy* (line 2). Use the following instructional sequence for teaching this word.

Say It: Revisit line 2 in the poem: *Whose dog was enormous and shaggy.* Highlight the word *shaggy* and say it together.

Define It: *Shaggy* describes something that is covered with long hair (or something like hair).

Explain It: My friend has a shaggy dog. She brushes his long fur every day.

Connect It: Tell why you might like to sit on a shaggy rug.

Say It Again: What's the word that means "covered with long hair?" (*shaggy*)

EXTENSIONS

DRAMATIC PLAY

Pet Groomers: Stock the dramatic play area with supplies (such as brushes, sponges, and shampoo) to inspire a pet-grooming business. Model conversation for different roles—for example, greeting customers and discussing their needs (groomer), and requesting a wash and trim for a shaggy dog (customer).

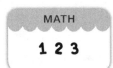
MATH
1 2 3

Carpet Sort: Collect carpet samples in different colors and textures for children to sort. As children sort the carpet samples, encourage them to use descriptive words (such as short, *long*, *soft*, *rough*, *shaggy*, *smooth*, *thick*, and *thin*) and to explain their sorting rules—for example, Shaggy/Not Shaggy.

More Words to Explore

Use the instructional sequence (left) as a model for exploring other words in the poem, such as:

young (line 1)
Reread line 1 and ask children how old Maggy might be. Reinforce that "young" means "having lived for a short time." Discuss that the opposite of *young* is *old*. Ask: *Do you think you are young or old? Why?*

enormous (line 2)
Share that if something is enormous, it is very big. Invite children to act out carrying something enormous, such as a watermelon.

vicious (line 4)
Explain that *vicious* means "wild or dangerous." This is a good opportunity to review safe behavior around animals. Ask: *Would it be safe to approach/pet a dog you do not know? Why or why not?*

Maggy's Dog

There was a young girl called Maggy,

Whose dog was enormous and shaggy.

The front end of him

Looked vicious and grim,

But the tail end was friendly and waggy.

— Author Unknown

The Silent Snake

Target Word: fluttering

SHARE THE POEM

Follow the guidelines on page 7 to share the poem "The Silent Snake." Invite children to pantomime the ways animals in the poem move. Review unfamiliar words or phrases. Let children know that a bough is another name for a tree branch. Share that mayflies are insects with wings.

EXPLORE WORD MEANINGS

Reread the poem and introduce the word *fluttering* (line 1). Use the following instructional sequence for teaching this word.

Say It: Revisit line 1 in the poem: *The birds go fluttering in the air.* Highlight the word *fluttering* and say it together.

Define It: If something is fluttering, it is moving or flying with very quick movements.

Explain It: The flag is fluttering in the wind today.

Connect It: If you saw leaves on a tree fluttering, what would you see?

Say It Again: What's the word that describes something that is moving or flying with very quick movements? (*fluttering*)

EXTENSIONS

DRAMATIC PLAY

Stage a Play: Create an audio recording of the poem. Guide children in selecting roles to play, including birds, rabbits, squirrels, mayflies, and one "silent snake." Have children take turns performing the parts of the fluttering birds.

MOVEMENT

Flutter Wands: Have children glue strips of crepe paper to one end of a 12-inch dowel (or paper-towel tube) to make "flutter wands." Invite them to explore ways to make the crepe paper flutter—for example, by gently waving the wand or twirling. Play "fluttery" music and let children use their wands to interpret what they hear.

More Words to Explore

Use the instructional sequence (left) as a model for exploring other words in the poem, such as:

dip (line 4)
Discuss what the mayflies are doing when they "dip," then let children share things they dip—for example, they might dip chips in salsa or dip their toes in water at the beach.

creatures (line 5)
Explain that creatures can be animals or people. Ask: *Which is not a creature: a robot, a baby, or a snake?*

silent (line 6)
Contrast the meaning of *silent* with *noisy*, then invite children to suggest times when it is important to be silent—for example, when someone is giving directions or there is a fire drill.

The Silent Snake

The birds go fluttering in the air.

The rabbits run and skip.

Brown squirrels race along the bough.

The mayflies rise and dip.

But while these creatures play and leap,

The silent snake goes *creepy-creep*!

— Author Unknown

Tadpoles

Target Word: cluster

SHARE THE POEM

Follow the guidelines on page 7 to share the poem "Tadpoles." As you read, invite children to imagine they are tadpoles changing into full-grown frogs. Let children share what they know about the life cycle of a frog. Display pictures of tadpoles and frogs. Which looks like a little fish? Which is the adult form?

EXPLORE WORD MEANINGS

Reread the poem and introduce the word *cluster* (line 2). Use the following instructional sequence for teaching this word.

Say It: Revisit lines 1 and 2 in the poem: *Tadpoles start as/ Clusters of eggs.* Highlight the word *clusters* and say it together.

Define It: *Cluster* describes a small group of things that are the same.

Explain It: My neighborhood is a cluster of houses, each with a small yard.

Connect It: If there is a cluster of apple trees in a field, what would you see?

Say It Again: What's the word that describes a small group of things that are the same? (*cluster*)

EXTENSIONS

BOOK SHARE

Frog (Watch Me Grow) **(DK, 2003):** Close-up, full-color photographs depict the life cycle of a frog—from a cluster of eggs to full-grown frogs.

DRAMATIC PLAY

Community Planners: Display photographs that depict examples of clusters in communities, such as a cluster of cottages by a lake, a cluster of trees in a field, a cluster of homes in a neighborhood, and a cluster of people waiting for a bus. Stock the center with blocks and other building materials, and let children create a community of clusters.

More Words to Explore

Use the instructional sequence (left) as a model for exploring other words in the poem, such as:

start (**line 1**)
Share that *start* means *begin*. Have fun practicing the meaning by giving children a start and stop signal to do something, such as dance, hum, or hop.

tails (**line 3**)
Let children locate tadpoles' tails in a picture. Ask: *What word sounds the same as "tail" but is the name for a story?* (tale)

croaking (**line 7**)
Invite children to croak like a frog. Then list other words for animal sounds, such as *bark, roar,* and *howl*. Invite children to illustrate the animals, then add sound words in speech bubbles.

Tadpoles

Tadpoles start as

Clusters of eggs . . .

Then heads and tails

And pretty soon legs.

Next thing you know

They all are on logs . . .

And croaking away

As full-grown frogs!

— Mary Sullivan

A White Hen Sitting

Target Word: squat

SHARE THE POEM

Follow the guidelines on page 7 to share the poem "A White Hen Sitting." Share background information about hens and chicks, including that chicks need to stay close to their mother for protection. In the poem, they hide beneath their mother's wing to stay safe from animals that might eat them.

EXPLORE WORD MEANINGS

Reread the poem and introduce the word *squat* (line 8). Use the following instructional sequence for teaching this word.

Say It:
Revisit lines 7 and 8 in the poem: *But chicks beneath their mother's wing/Squat safe as safe can be.* Highlight the word *squat* and say it together.

Define It:
When people squat, they sit on their heels or crouch with their knees bent.

Explain It:
I spilled milk on the floor and had to squat to wipe it up.

Connect It:
Can you squat on the rug? Show me.

Say It Again:
What word describes sitting on your heels with your knees bent? (*squat*)

EXTENSIONS

MATH
1 2 3

Chicks and Hens: Set up a math center with cutouts of chicks and hens. On hens, write the following sentence frame:

_____ *chicks beneath their mother's wing*

Squat safe as safe can be.

Make number cards sized to fit in the blank. Have children choose a number card to complete the sentence, then count out chicks to place with the hen.

MOVEMENT

Make a Move: Gather children in an open area and lead them in a sequence of movements that includes squats—for example, *squat, stand, hop,* and *skip.*

More Words to Explore

Use the instructional sequence (left) as a model for exploring other words in the poem, such as:

speckled **(line 3)**
Ask: *What is speckled in the poem?* (eggs) Share pictures of speckled eggs to help children understand the meaning. Recite the familiar nursery rhyme "Five Little Speckled Frogs" with children to have fun using the word.

plump **(line 4)**
Explain that *plump* means "full and round." Ask: *Would you like to put your head on a plump pillow or a flat pillow? Why?*

beneath **(line 7)**
Share that *beneath* means "to be right under something." Let children describe items in the classroom that are beneath something—for example, "My cubby is beneath Kimiko's cubby."

A White Hen Sitting

A white hen sitting

On white eggs three:

Next, three speckled chickens

As plump as plump can be.

An owl, and a hawk,

And a bat come to see:

But chicks beneath their mother's wing

Squat safe as safe can be.

— Christina Rossetti

Dandelion

Target Word: glistened

SHARE THE POEM

Follow the guidelines on page 7 to share the poem "Dandelion." Invite children to pretend they are holding a dandelion and blowing the seeds away. Review unfamiliar words or phrases. For example, reread lines 7 and 8 ("And, sad to tell! Her charming hair/Blew many miles away."). Ask: *What do you think really blew away?*

EXPLORE WORD MEANINGS

Reread the poem and introduce the word *glistened* (line 3). Use the following instructional sequence for teaching this word.

Say It: Revisit lines 1 through 3 in the poem: *There was a pretty dandelion/With lovely, fluffy hair,/That glistened in the sunshine.* Highlight the word *glistened* and say it together.

Define It: When something glistens, it gives off a sparkling light.

Explain It: I remember walking home on a winter night. The snow glistened in the moonlight.

Connect It: If leaves glistened after a rain shower, what would you see?

Say It Again: What's the word that describes when something gives off a sparkling light? (*glistens*)

EXTENSIONS

ART

Glistening Cards: Have children cut out pictures of flowers from magazines, glue them to blank cards, then dot with glitter glue. Let dry, then have children write or dictate a note to someone special.

BOOK SHARE

Deep Nature: Photographs From Iowa by **John Pearson (University of Iowa Press, 2009):** Take a picture walk with children through this stunning collection of photographs for examples of the way nature glistens in dewdrops, flowers, insects, and more.

More Words to Explore

Use the instructional sequence (left) as a model for exploring other words in the poem, such as:

fluffy (**line 2**)
Let children explore fluffy objects, such as cotton balls, plush animals, and fleece. Ask: *Are some fluffier than others? Which one is the fluffiest?*

charming (**line 7**)
Explain that *charming* means "delightful." Discuss why the poet may have described the dandelion seeds this way. Then let children take turns describing something they find charming.

blew (**line 8**)
Review the meaning of *blew*, then ask: *What word sounds like this but names a color?* (blue) Review that *blew* and *blue* sound the same but have different spellings and meanings.

Dandelion

There was a pretty dandelion

With lovely, fluffy hair,

That glistened in the sunshine

And in the summer air.

But oh! This pretty dandelion

Soon grew old and grey;

And, sad to tell! Her charming hair

Blew many miles away.

— Author Unknown

I Am an Oak

Target Word: mighty

SHARE THE POEM

Follow the guidelines on page 7 to share the poem "I Am an Oak." Explain that an oak is a large tree and that the seeds of an oak tree are called acorns. They look like little heads with caps on top.

EXPLORE WORD MEANINGS

Reread the poem and introduce the word *mighty* (line 2). Use the following instructional sequence for teaching this word.

Say It: Revisit lines 1 and 2 in the poem: *I am an oak,/a mighty tree.* Highlight the word *mighty* and say it together.

Define It: Mighty means "very strong, powerful, or big."

Explain It: I went for a bike ride yesterday and it took a mighty effort to get up the big hill near my house!

Connect It: Tell me about a favorite storybook or cartoon character you think is mighty.

Say It Again: What's the word that describes something that is very big or strong? (*mighty*)

EXTENSIONS

MATH
1 2 3

Mighty Measurements: Share that oak trees can grow to be more than 100 feet tall. Take children to a hallway (or outside) to find out what 100 feet looks like. In advance, use cones (or other markers) to mark a 100-foot length. Help children measure and cut pieces of string that are 10 feet long. Have children predict how many pieces of string equal 100 feet, then lay them end to end to find out.

MOVEMENT

Mighty and Mini Steps: Lead children in taking mighty and mini steps as they put away materials, take a movement break between lessons, or line up to leave or return from for lunch, recess, or other activities. For example, say "Take three mighty steps . . . [five mini steps, six mighty steps, and so on]."

More Words to Explore

Use the instructional sequence (left) as a model for exploring other words in the poem, such as:

oak (**line 1**)
Display a photo of an oak tree. Have children name other kinds of trees (such as *pine, elm,* and *maple*).

cap (**line 4**)
Compare a cap to other types of hats, then have children help make a list of things people wear on their heads—for example, berets, scarves, crowns, and helmets.

tall (**line 5**)
Explain that something that is tall is very high. Collect and display pictures of things that are tall, such as skyscrapers, trees, ladders, and flagpoles.

I Am an Oak

I am an oak,

a mighty tree,

I grew from an acorn, small;

with a tiny cap, and a tiny stem—

who knew I'd grow so tall?

— Helen H. Moore

Quiet Seeds

Target Word: precious

SHARE THE POEM

Follow the guidelines on page 7 to share the poem "Quiet Seeds." Invite children to pantomime the actions of a growing plant. Review unfamiliar words or phrases. For example, reread line 5 ("Quiet seeds are waking."), then ask: *What do you think is happening? How is this like waking up?*

EXPLORE WORD MEANINGS

Reread the poem and introduce the word *precious* (line 3). Use the following instructional sequence for teaching this word.

Say It: Revisit lines 3 and 4 in the poem: *Patient, precious promises/Waiting just to grow.* Highlight the word *precious* and say it together.

Define It: *Precious* describes something that is very special.

Explain It: Zoey is our new puppy. She is our precious pet.

Connect It: Who or what is precious to you? Why?

Say It Again: What's the word that means "very special?" (*precious*)

EXTENSIONS

BOOK SHARE

Welcome, Precious **by Nikki Grimes (Orchard, 2006):** Poetic text captures the precious moments of a new baby's arrival. Revisit pages in the book with children and invite them to share their favorite precious moments.

SCIENCE

State Stones: Explore your state's natural resources, including gems, rocks, and stones. If there is an official state stone, do research to determine if it is a "precious stone." Extend learning by discussing other natural resources, such as water, plants, animals, and trees. Help children to develop an understanding of why our natural resources are "precious" and what people can do to protect them.

More Words to Explore

Use the instructional sequence (left) as a model for exploring other words in the poem, such as:

resting (line 2)
Explain that if someone is resting, he or she is sleeping or relaxing. Ask: *Do you think it would be easy to rest in a noisy restaurant? Why or why not?*

patient (line 3)
Compare the meaning of *patient* and *impatient*. Look for opportunities throughout the day to compliment children on being patient.

stretch (line 7)
Reread the poem, inviting children to act out being seeds that are waking up and "searching for the sun." Have them "stretch out" as their stems, leaves, and roots grow.

Quiet Seeds

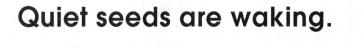

Quiet seeds are sleeping.

They're resting in a row.

Patient, precious promises

Waiting just to grow.

Quiet seeds are waking.

They're searching for the sun.

Stems and leaves and roots stretch out.

The magic has begun.

— Jodi Simpson

Strawberries

Target Word: pluck

SHARE THE POEM

Follow the guidelines on page 7 to share the poem "Strawberries." Invite children to use hand movements that correspond to action words: *pluck*, *pinch*, *twist*, *put it in a cup*, and *eat it up*. Let children know that strawberries are grown in fields or gardens. Strawberries are ready to pick when they are bright red.

EXPLORE WORD MEANINGS

Reread the poem and introduce the word *pluck* (line 5). Use the following instructional sequence for teaching this word.

Say It: Revisit line 5 in the poem: *Pluck the berry.*
Highlight the word *pluck* and say it together.

Define It: *Pluck* means "to pull or pick something."

Explain It: When I see weeds in my garden, I pluck them.

Connect It: Show me how you would pluck an apple from a tree.

Say It Again: What's the word that means "to pull or pick something?" (*pluck*)

EXTENSIONS

MOVEMENT

Feather Ball: Stick feathers into a foam ball for this version of Wonder Ball. As children pass the "feather ball" around a circle, have them recite the rhyme (below). Each time a child plucks a feather, begin again.

> *The feather ball goes round and round.*
> *To pass it quickly you are bound.*
> *If you're the one to hold it last,*
> *Pluck a feather, and the game is past.*

SCIENCE

String Sounds: Provide a hands-on opportunity to explore the word *pluck*. Provide empty containers (such as shoe boxes without the lids), and help children stretch large rubber bands over the openings. Their string instruments are ready to pluck!

More Words to Explore

Use the instructional sequence (left) as a model for exploring other words in the poem, such as:

leafy (line 4)
Invite children to suggest leafy greens they can eat, such as spinach, lettuce, and bok choy. Plan a tasting! (Remember to check for food allergies.)

sun (line 6)
Review that the sun is a star. Ask: *Do you know another word that sounds the same but refers to a male child?* (son) *Are you a son or daughter?* Review that these words sound the same but have different spellings and meanings.

twist (line 9)
Let children act out uses of this word—for example, twist a lid off a jar, twist a tie to close a bag, and "do the twist!"

Strawberries

Plump strawberries.

Ripe strawberries.

Bright red heart-shaped strawberries,

Hiding under leafy greens.

Pluck the berry

In the summer sun.

Pinch the stem.

Have some fun.

Twist the stem,

Almost done.

Put the berry

In a cup.

Better yet,

Just eat it up!

— Beth Sycamore

Sunflowers

Target Word: hollow

SHARE THE POEM

Follow the guidelines on page 7 to share the poem "Sunflowers." Invite children to recall interesting words in the poem that help them picture what a sunflower looks like. Share that sunflowers can grow to more than 20 feet tall!

EXPLORE WORD MEANINGS

Reread the poem and introduce the word *hollow* (line 5). Use the following instructional sequence for teaching this word. (See also "Underground Rumbling," page 60 for another look at the word *hollow*.)

Say It: Revisit line 5 in the poem: *Tall hollow stems.* Highlight the word *hollow* and say it together.

Define It: If something is hollow, it has an empty space inside.

Explain It: There's a long hollow tube in our playground. It's lots of fun to crawl through.

Connect It: Do you think it would be easy or difficult to move a hollow log? Tell me why.

Say It Again: What's the word that describes something that has an empty space inside? (*hollow*)

EXTENSIONS

ART

Hollow Tube Sculptures: Stock the art center with assorted cardboard tubes. (Precut some into different sizes.) Invite children to use the tubes to create sculptures, using glue or tape to connect the pieces.

SCIENCE

Tree-Hollow Habitats: Share that sunflowers have strong but hollow stems to hold up big blooms. Introduce another example of the word *hollow*: a tree hollow. Investigate animals that make their homes in tree hollows, including birds.

More Words to Explore

Use the instructional sequence (left) as a model for exploring other words in the poem, such as:

shiny (line 4)
Explain that if something is shiny, it gives off a lot of light. Invite children to imagine they spot something shiny on the ground. What could it be? (See "Before the Bath," page 14, for a related lesson.)

arranged (line 6)
Demonstrate the meaning of this word by letting children help you arrange books on a bookshelf in a particular way, such as by size or alphabetical order.

row (line 7)
Discuss the use of *row* in the poem, then notice examples of rows in the classroom, such as rows of chairs, boxes on the calendar, and cubbies.

Sunflowers

I saw—

Bright yellow petals

Round flower heads

Long shiny leaves

Tall hollow stems.

All arranged

neatly in a row

In my backyard.

— Beth Sycamore

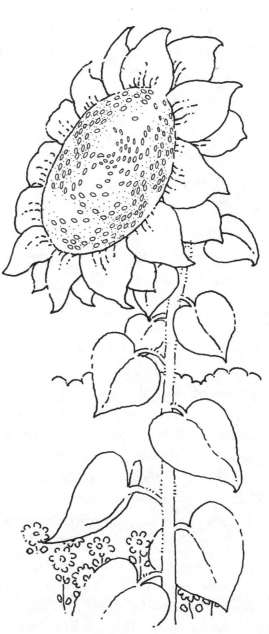

Autumn Leaves

Target Word: twirl

SHARE THE POEM

Follow the guidelines on page 7 to share the poem "Autumn Leaves." As you read, invite children to imagine they are leaves, fluttering and falling quietly to the ground. Review that "autumn" is another name for "fall." It is the season that comes between summer and winter. Encourage children to share things they like to do or see in autumn.

EXPLORE WORD MEANINGS

Reread the poem and introduce the word *twirl* (line 3). Use the following instructional sequence for teaching this word.

Say It: Revisit line 3 in the poem: *They whirl, they twirl, they dance.* Highlight the word *twirl* and say it together.

Define It: *Twirl* means "to spin around."

Explain It: When I eat spaghetti, I twirl the spaghetti on my fork.

Connect It: Show me how you can twirl around the room.

Say It Again: What's the word that means "to spin around?" (*twirl*)

EXTENSIONS

ART

Sparkle and Twirl: Make sparkly spinners that twirl in the breeze. Draw two-inch spirals on paper plates. Let each child decorate a plate, adding glitter glue as a finishing touch. Help children cut the plates into spirals and punch a hole at the center. Tie on string, then hang the spinners where they will catch a little wind and twirl, for instance in the school's entryway.

WRITING

How to Eat Spaghetti: Give each child a fork and an imaginary bowl of spaghetti. As children twirl the "noodles" on their forks, work together to write instructions for how to eat spaghetti—for example, "First you pick up the fork. Next you put the fork into the spaghetti. You twirl the fork to wrap some noodles around it. Then you put the fork in your mouth and eat the spaghetti!"

More Words to Explore

Use the instructional sequence (left) as a model for exploring other words in the poem, such as:

whirl (line 3)
Explain that *whirl* means "to turn around quickly." Invite children to act out the word when they hear a specific signal, such as three claps or two stomps.

whisper (line 6)
Let children demonstrate the word *whisper* by using very quiet voices with each other. Discuss times when it is a good idea to whisper.

pile (line 7)
Review that in the poem, leaves pile up as they fall. Ask: *What are some other piles of things?* (for example, a pile of laundry or a pile of papers)

Autumn Leaves

Autumn leaves, they flutter

As they fall down to the ground.

They whirl, they twirl, they dance,

But they don't make a sound.

Quiet, oh-so-quiet,

They whisper on their way,

Landing in a pile

In which we all can play.

— Jodi Simpson

Frost

Target Word: swirls

SHARE THE POEM

Follow the guidelines on page 7 to share the poem "Frost." As you read, invite children to pantomime actions, such as drawing, dancing, and gliding. Review unfamiliar words or phrases. For example, explain that etching is similar to drawing. Allow time for children to describe places they have seen frost, such as on windows, grass, even on food coming out of the freezer.

EXPLORE WORD MEANINGS

Reread the poem and introduce the word *swirls* (line 3). Use the following instructional sequence for teaching this word.

Say It: Revisit line 3 in the poem: *etching swirls while I sleep.* Highlight the word *swirls* and say it together.

Define It: A swirl is something that winds around in a curving or spiraling way.

Explain It: The water in my kitchen sink circles around the drain in swirls when I pull the plug.

Connect It: Tell me what happens when you stir a glass of lemonade or a cup of cocoa. Do you make a swirl?

Say It Again: What word describes things that wind around in a curving or spiraling way? (*swirls*)

EXTENSIONS

ART

Frosty Swirls: Let children etch swirls of "frost" on a cookie-sheet "window." Cover a cookie sheet with shaving cream. Have children use craft sticks, the end of a paintbrush, or other tools to draw swirls. Smooth it out and repeat.

BOOK SHARE

Here Comes Jack Frost by Kazuno Kohara **(Roaring Book Press, 2009):** Spare but striking illustrations invite readers along on an enchanting winter adventure.

More Words to Explore

Use the instructional sequence (left) as a model for exploring other words in the poem, such as:

artist (**line 1**)
Discuss what an artist does—for example, creates paintings and drawings. Make a list of tools and materials artists use.

gliding (**line 5**)
Share that someone who is gliding, such as a skater, is moving smoothly and quietly. Ask: *What kinds of animals glide?* (See page 58, "That One's Me," for a lesson on the word *glide*.)

view (**line 6**)
Explain that a *view* is what you see from a certain place. Look out a window with children. Invite them to describe the view.

Frost

Frost is an artist

drawing on my window,

etching swirls while I sleep.

Frost is a skater

dancing, gliding on glass,

changing my outside view.

Frost is a dream,

telling fairy tales

in winter white.

—Kathleen M. Hollenbeck

Splash

Target Word: trickled

SHARE THE POEM

Follow the guidelines on page 7 to share the poem "Splash." Discuss the poem, inviting children to share rainy day experiences. Ask: *What are some things you see on a rainy day? What do you like to do on a rainy day? How does rain feel?*

EXPLORE WORD MEANINGS

Reread the poem and introduce the word *trickled* (line 4). Use the following instructional sequence for teaching this word.

Say It: Revisit lines 3 and 4 in the poem: *"Splash," said another/ As it trickled down my back.* Highlight the word *trickled* and say it together.

Define It: *Trickle* means "to fall or move slowly in little drops or small amounts."

Explain It: Water was trickling from my faucet, so I had to get it fixed.

Connect It: What might you trickle on pancakes?

Say It Again: What's the word that means "to fall slowly in little drops or small amounts?" (*trickle*)

EXTENSIONS

BOOK SHARE

***Listen to the Rain* by Bill Martin Jr. and John Archambault (Henry Holt, 1988):** A magical combination of rhythmic text and stunning watercolors captures the sights and sounds of a rainy day.

SCIENCE

A Trickle Experiment: Set up a science station with tubs of water, droppers, spoons, and assorted containers (including squirt bottles). Let children experiment with making water trickle. Make a real-life connection by discussing why some foods, such as ketchup, come in certain kinds of containers and not others. Encourage use of the word *trickle* in related conversations.

More Words to Explore

Use the instructional sequence (left) as a model for exploring other words in the poem, such as:

back (line 4)
Let children point to their back. Broaden children's understanding by using the word in different ways—for example, ask: *Where do you like to sit on the bus: in the front or in the back?*

rude (line 5)
Explain that the opposite of *rude* is *polite*. Ask: *What is an example of a rude behavior? What is something you can do that is polite?*

splashed (line 7)
Invite children to take turns sharing an experience in which something was splashed—for example, *The bus went through the puddle in the road and splashed water all over us!*

Splash

"Splash," said a raindrop

As it fell upon my hat;

"Splash," said another

As it trickled down my back.

"You are very rude," I said

As I looked up to the sky;

Then another raindrop splashed

Right into my eye!

— Author Unknown

Spring

Target Word: chirping

SHARE THE POEM

Follow the guidelines on page 7 to share the poem "Spring." Invite children to describe signs of spring they notice, such as warmer days, leaf buds on trees, and the "cheer-up" sound of a robin. Discuss changes in what people wear as the weather gets warmer. For example, children may put away warm winter coats and wear lighter jackets.

EXPLORE WORD MEANINGS

Reread the poem and introduce the word *chirping* (line 5). Use the following instructional sequence for teaching this word.

Say It: Revisit line 5 in the poem: *Birds chirping is one more reason.* Highlight the word *chirping* and say it together.

Define It: When you hear a bird or insect chirp, you hear a short, high-pitched sound.

Explain It: Sometimes at night, I hear a cricket chirping outside my window. *Chirp. Chirp. Chirp.*

Connect It: Tell me about birds or insects you hear chirping.

Say It Again: What's the word that describes a short, high-pitched sound? (*chirp*)

EXTENSIONS

BOOK SHARE

Wild Birds by Joanne Ryder (HarperCollins, 2003): Poetic text invites readers to "look and listen" as they observe birds all around—"swirling through the air" and "speckling the treetops." Make a connection to birds children see and hear in the world outside the classroom. What do they think birds are communicating when they chirp?

DRAMATIC PLAY

Birdwatchers: Create a dramatic play area that invites children to take a bird-watching walk. Set the scene with pictures of birds and props, such as water bottles, backpacks, binoculars, and journals (for recording observations). Prompt conversations about the birds children hear "chirping."

More Words to Explore

Use the instructional sequence (left) as a model for exploring other words in the poem, such as:

flowers (line 2)
Let children share their favorite flower, then ask: *What is a word that sounds the same as* flower *but is the name for an ingredient people use to make bread?* (flour) Review that these words sound the same but have different spellings and meanings.

adore (line 4)
Explain that *adore* means to like something or someone a lot. Let children use the word to tell about someone or something they adore.

reason (line 5)
Discuss the meaning of this word. Then let children share their favorite season and the reasons they "adore" that season.

Spring

Signs of spring, more each day

Rain in April, flowers in May

T-shirts and shorts come out once more

Spring is the season I adore

Birds chirping is one more reason

That I love, love, love this season.

— Vince Novelli

Summer Memories

Target Word: ripples

SHARE THE POEM

Follow the guidelines on page 7 to share the poem "Summer Memories." Display the poem and guide children to notice that the letters that begin lines 1–6 spell the word *summer*. Invite children to make connections to the poem, sharing their own summer memories.

EXPLORE WORD MEANINGS

Reread the poem and introduce the word *ripples* (line 6). Use the following instructional sequence for teaching this word.

Say It: Revisit lines 6 and 7 in the poem: *Ripples on my grandma's lake/as we splash and shout.* Highlight the word *ripples* and say it together.

Define It: A ripple is a small wave.

Explain It: When I throw a stone into a lake, it makes ripples.

Connect It: Do you think a duck would make a ripple on a pond?

Say It Again: What's the word that means "a small wave?" (*ripple*)

EXTENSIONS

BOOK SHARE

Canoe Days by Gary Paulsen (Doubleday, 1999): Lush illustrations and lyrical text transport readers to a lake for a peaceful canoe trip.

SCIENCE

Making Ripples: Cover an open area on the floor with a cloth (or newspaper) and place a large tub of water at the center. Display an assortment of small rocks. Have children predict what will happen when you drop a rock into the water. Make a chart to document children's suggestions. Drop the rock and let children share observations. Let children take turns repeating the activity with different-sized rocks and compare results.

More Words to Explore

Use the instructional sequence (left) as a model for exploring other words in the poem, such as:

slippery (line 1)
Share that something that is slippery is smooth and/or wet. Discuss what makes a kayak slippery (*water*). Let children show how they would hold onto something slippery.

kayaks (line 1)
Explain that a kayak is a type of boat. Invite children to look through magazines to find pictures of kayaks and other types of boats. Use the images to create a picture/word web.

shout (line 7)
Let children share experiences when they have needed to shout to get someone's attention. Discuss words with similar meanings, such as *yell*, *scream*, or *bellow*.

Summer Memories

Slippery tipsy kayaks

Underwater somersaults

Misty morning hikes

Millions of mosquitoes

Empty bottles of sunscreen

Ripples on my grandma's lake

 as we splash and shout.

— Beth Sycamore

Cloud Gazing

Target Word: willowy

SHARE THE POEM

Follow the guidelines on page 7 to share the poem "Cloud Gazing." As you read, invite children to imagine they are looking up at the sky. Have children recall interesting words and phrases that help them picture the clouds—for example, in line 6, "Flat as a pancake."

EXPLORE WORD MEANINGS

Reread the poem and introduce the word *willowy* (line 3). Use the following instructional sequence for teaching this word.

Say It: Revisit lines 1 through 5 in the poem: *Light clouds/Dark clouds/Willowy/Billowy/Thunderclouds.* Highlight the word *willowy* and say it together.

Define It: *Willowy* means "tall, thin, and graceful."

Explain It: I enjoyed watching the willowy dancers as they moved across the stage.

Connect It: Tell me what you might see if you were looking at a willowy tree.

Say It Again: What's the word that means "tall, thin, and graceful?" (*willowy*)

EXTENSIONS

BOOK SHARE

Clouds by Anne Rockwell (Collins, 2008): This informative book in the Lets-Read-and-Find-Out Science series describes clouds and changes in weather that are associated with them.

DRAMATIC PLAY

Cloud Forecasters: Transform the dramatic play area into a weather station for recording observations about clouds and forecasting the weather. A few simple props—such as microphones, old cameras, and an umbrella—will encourage "on-scene" reporting. Guide children to connect the types of clouds they observe with the weather they predict— for example, "Those willowy clouds we're seeing are expected to bring fair weather today."

More Words to Explore

Use the instructional sequence (left) as a model for exploring other words in the poem, such as:

flat (line 6)
Have children point out examples of things that are flat and things that are uneven (or not flat). Work with children to define the word. (*not deep; smooth and even*)

milky (line 8)
Have children describe the color of milk, then look for things around the room that are milky in color.

silky (line 9)
Share scraps of silky fabrics. Ask: *Would a silky shirt feel good to wear? Why?*

Cloud Gazing

Light clouds

Dark clouds

Willowy

Billowy

Thunderclouds

Flat as a pancake

Tall as a tower

Milky

Silky

Silver white clouds

— Beth Sycamore

Goodnight, Sun

Target Word: perch

SHARE THE POEM

Follow the guidelines on page 7 to share the poem "Goodnight, Sun." Invite children to describe colors they see in the sky when the sun sets. Review unfamiliar words or phrases. For example, reread lines 5 and 6 ("And at sunset it pauses, to tell us goodnight"). Ask: *Does the sun really say goodnight? What do you think is happening here? How is this like when you go to bed?*

EXPLORE WORD MEANINGS

Reread the poem and introduce the word *perch* (line 3). Use the following instructional sequence for teaching this word.

Say It: Revisit lines 1 through 4 in the poem: *The sun slides down/the west of the sky,/from the perch it held/at noon, so high.* Highlight the word *perch* and say it together.

Define It: A perch is a raised place where something or someone can sit or rest.

Explain It: The fence in my yard makes a good perch for the birds.

Connect It: What do you see outside that could be a perch for a bird?

Say It Again: What is the word that describes a raised place where something or someone can sit or rest? (*perch*)

EXTENSIONS

MOVEMENT

Setting Sun: Reread the poem, this time inviting children to imagine they are the sun, sliding down from their "perch" high in the sky, then pausing to say "goodnight" as they curl up on the floor and pretend to go to sleep.

WRITING

A Perch for Me: Discuss perches for people and animals. For example, a ladder is a perch for a painter and a windowsill is a perch for a cat. Invite children to use their imaginations to complete and illustrate this sentence frame: *From my perch on _____ , I see _____ .*

More Words to Explore

Use the instructional sequence (left) as a model for exploring other words in the poem, such as:

noon (line 4)
Check the class schedule. What are children doing at noon? Point out that 12:00 P.M. is the same as *noon*. Discuss other words for times of the day, such as *morning*, *afternoon*, and *evening*.

pauses (line 5)
Explain that *pause* means to stop doing something for a short time. Use the word with children as you pause during the day—for example, to answer a question.

light (line 8)
Discuss sources of light, such as the sun, a lamp, and a flashlight. Ask: *What word sounds the same and describes something that is not heavy* (light). *Is your backpack heavy or light?*

Goodnight, Sun

The sun slides down

the west of the sky,

from the perch it held

at noon, so high.

And at sunset it pauses,

to tell us goodnight,

as it turns off the daytime,

then turns out the light.

— Helen H. Moore

I'm Glad the Sky Is Painted Blue

Target Word: sandwiched

SHARE THE POEM

Follow the guidelines on page 7 to share the poem "I'm Glad the Sky Is Painted Blue." Ask questions to guide a discussion—for example: *Is the sky really painted blue? The earth painted green? Why do you think the poet describes the sky and earth this way? How are the sky, air, and earth like a sandwich?*

EXPLORE WORD MEANINGS

Reread the poem and introduce the word *sandwiched* (line 4). Use the following instructional sequence for teaching this word.

Say It: Revisit lines 3 and 4 in the poem: *With such a lot of nice fresh air/All sandwiched in between.* Highlight the word *sandwiched* and say it together.

Define It: *Sandwiched* means "to be between two people or things."

Explain It: Sometimes I like to change the pillows on my couch. I sandwiched a bright red pillow between two white ones.

Connect It: Tell me who you were sandwiched between in line today.

Say It Again: What's the word that means "to be between two people or things?" (*sandwiched*)

EXTENSIONS

DRAMATIC PLAY

Sandwich Shop: Work with children to transform the dramatic play area into a sandwich shop: Cut paper, yarn, and fabric scraps to make fillings, old file folders to make sliced bread, and brown bags to make tortillas and wraps. Add plates, napkins, empty (and clean!) condiment bottles, and order pads.

MATH

1 2 3

If You Are… Play a quick "line-up" game that promotes listening and following directions (and reinforces the word *sandwiched*, in this case). Use the following script as a model: *If you are third in line, clap two times. If you are sandwiched between [name] and [name], raise your hand.* Continue, giving each child a chance to participate.

More Words to Explore

Use the instructional sequence (left) as a model for exploring other words in the poem, such as:

glad (line 1)
Let children share something they are glad about, then discuss words with a similar meaning, such as *happy* and *delighted*.

sky (line 1)
Brainstorm things children can see in the sky, such as birds, clouds, and airplanes. Record their words on a sky-blue wall chart.

fresh (line 3)
Discuss the importance of fresh air. Ask: *What other things are good when they are fresh?* (for example, fruits and vegetables)

I'm Glad the Sky Is Painted Blue

I'm glad the sky is painted blue,

And the earth is painted green,

With such a lot of nice fresh air

All sandwiched in between.

— Author Unknown

A Starry Zoo

Target Word: flicker

SHARE THE POEM

Follow the guidelines on page 7 to share the poem "A Starry Zoo." Discuss the poem, inviting children to share what they know about lions, hares, swans, and bears. Ask: *Do you think these animals are really in the sky?* Share that some groups of stars, called constellations, seem to form shapes or pictures in the sky—like the animals in the poem. Share pictures of constellations to enhance understanding.

EXPLORE WORD MEANINGS

Reread the poem and introduce the word *flicker* (line 5). Use the following instructional sequence for teaching this word.

Say It: Revisit lines 5 and 6 in the poem: *Flicker up high/in the night sky.* Highlight the word *flicker* and say it together.

Define It: If a light flickers, it is not steady.

Explain It: It's fun to watch fireflies as they flicker in the dark.

Connect It: Describe what you might see if the flame on a birthday candle flickers.

Say It Again: What's the word that describes light that is not steady? (*flicker*)

EXTENSIONS

Things That Flicker: Talk about things children might see flickering in the dark, such as stars, fireflies, and lights. Have children paint a sheet of paper dark blue and let dry, then dab on glitter glue to create flickering objects at night.

Zoo in the Sky: A Book of Animal Constellations **by Jacqueline Mitton (National Geographic Children's Books, 2006):** Shiny foil stars form animal shapes in this informative book about constellations.

More Words to Explore

Use the instructional sequence (left) as a model for exploring other words in the poem, such as:

swift (line 2)
A swift hare is a fast hare. Invite children to be swift when they get ready for an activity.

sly (line 2)
Sly means "sneaky." Discuss words with a similar meaning, such as *tricky*, *clever*, and *cunning*. Share a story that features a sly character, such as the wolf in *Little Red Riding Hood* or the fox in *The Gingerbread Boy.*

curious (line 4)
Someone who is curious wants to learn more about something. Let children share something they are curious about.

A Starry Zoo

A fierce brave lion

A swift, sly hare

A majestic swan

A curious bear

Flicker up high

in the night sky.

— Beth Sycamore

Under the Ground

Target Word: snuggle

SHARE THE POEM

Follow the guidelines on page 7 to share the poem "Under the Ground." Allow time for children to make connections between the poem and their own experiences digging in the ground. Recall words that describe how the ground feels. (*cool and wet*) Discuss interesting words or phrases. For example, reread lines 9 and 10 ("Do they hear us walking/On the grass above their heads"). Ask: *What do you imagine the worms and ants and bugs are doing under the ground as we move above them?*

EXPLORE WORD MEANINGS

Reread the poem and introduce the word *snuggle* (line 12). Use the following instructional sequence for teaching this word.

Say It: Revisit lines 11 and 12 in the poem: *Hear us running over/ While they snuggle in their beds?* Highlight the word *snuggle* and say it together.

Define It: *Snuggle* means "to hold something very close."

Explain It: After a long day, I like to snuggle on the couch with my daughter. It's so cozy.

Connect It: Do you snuggle with something special when you go to sleep? Tell me about it.

Say It Again: What's the word that means "to hold something very close?" (*snuggle*)

EXTENSIONS

Snuggle Buddies: Bring in old woolly mittens. Have children push the thumbs in, then fill the mittens with pillow stuffing. Help them stitch the opening closed. Then let them use felt, ribbons, and other embellishments to make faces on their snuggle buddies.

What Is Snuggly? Collect pictures of snuggly things, such as teddy bears and blankets. Glue the pictures to mural paper and add a title: *What is snuggly? Snuggly is* … Label the pictures to complete a display that will expand children's understanding of this word.

More Words to Explore

Use the instructional sequence (left) as a model for exploring other words in the poem, such as:

softly (**line 7**)
Explain that *softly* means "in a quiet or gentle way." To extend understanding, ask: *If music were softly playing in our room, do you think it would bother people in other classrooms? Why or why not?*

round (**line 7**)
Explain that *round* is short for "around"—the ants and bugs are creeping *around* the stones and rocks. Let children act out going softly "round" the classroom.

pushing (**line 8**)
Share that when you push something, you make it move. Have children suggest things we can push—for example, a button in an elevator, a shopping cart, and a swing.

Under the Ground

What is under the grass,
Way down in the ground,
Where everything is cool and wet
With darkness all around?

Little pink worms live there;
Ants and brown bugs creep
Softly round the stones and rocks
Where roots are pushing deep.

Do they hear us walking
On the grass above their heads;
Hear us running over
While they snuggle in their beds?

— Rhoda W. Bacmeister

Acknowledgments

All About Me

"Before the Bath" by Corinna Marsh from *Read-Aloud Rhymes for the Very Young* (Knopf, 1986).

"Fearless" by Kathleen M. Hollenbeck. Copyright © 2010 by Kathleen M. Hollenbeck. Used by permission of the author.

"Haircut" by Mary Sullivan from *101 Thematic Poems for Emergent Readers* (Scholastic, 1999). Copyright © 1999 by Mary Sullivan. Used by permission of the author.

"My Loose Tooth" by Ruth Kanarek is reprinted from *Poetry Place Anthology*. Copyright © 1990 by Scholastic Inc. Used by permission of the publisher.

Colors

"The Color Yellow" by Brendan Nixon is reprinted from *A Poem for Every Day!* (Scholastic, 2006) by permission of Sid Reischer.

"Flower Boxes" by Jean Brabham McKinney is reprinted from *Poetry Place Anthology*. Copyright © 1990 by Scholastic Inc. Used by permission of the publisher.

"My Park" and "A Rainbow of Colors" by Beth Sycamore. Copyright © 2010 by Beth Sycamore.

"Sidewalk Art" by Jenny Whitehead is reprinted from *Lunch Box Mail and Other Poems*. Copyright © 2001 by Jenny Whitehead. Published by Henry Holt and Co.

Food

"Beans, Beans, Beans" by Lucia and James L. Hymes, Jr. from *Hooray for Chocolate and Other Easy to Read Jingles*.

"Carrots" by Beth Sycamore. Copyright © 2010 by Beth Sycamore.

"How Many Ways to Say Cooking" by Kiki Camerota is reprinted from *A Poem for Every Day!* (Scholastic, 2006) by permission of Sid Reischer.

"Pizza Pizzazz" by Liza Charlesworth from *A Poem a Day* (Scholastic, 1997). Used by permission of the author.

Neighborhoods

"The Corner Store," "The Mail Carrier," "Monkey Bars," and "Street Sweeper" by Beth Sycamore. Copyright © 2010 by Beth Sycamore.

"Music" by Caitlin Mahar is reprinted from *A Poem for Every Day!* (Scholastic, 2006) by permission of Sid Reischer.

Transportation

"City Bus" and "On My Scooter" by Beth Sycamore. Copyright © 2010 by Beth Sycamore.

"Night Trucks" by Thelma Ireland is reprinted from *Poetry Place Anthology*. Copyright © 1990 by Scholastic Inc. Used by permission of the publisher.

"That One's Me" by Tony Mitton is reprinted from *First Verses* (Oxford University Press, 1997). Copyright © 1996 by Tony Mitton.

"Underground Rumbling" by James S. Tippett is reprinted from *Crickety Cricket! The Best Loved Poems of James S. Tippett*. Copyright © 1973 by Martha K. Tippett. Published by HarperCollins.

Creepy, Crawly Critters

"Beetles in the Garden" by Elsie S. Lindgren is reprinted from *Poetry Place Anthology*. Copyright © 1990 by Scholastic Inc. Used by permission of the publisher.

"Busy Bee" by Kathleen M. Hollenbeck from *The Big Book of Classroom Poems* (Scholastic, 2004). Copyright © 2004 by Kathleen M. Hollenbeck. Used by permission of the author.

"Tiny World" by Mary Sullivan from *101 Thematic Poems for Emergent Readers* (Scholastic, 1999). Copyright © 1999 by Mary Sullivan. Used by permission of the author.

Animals

"Crocodile" by Katie Touff from *A Poem a Day* (Scholastic, 1997). Used by permission of the publisher.

"Tadpoles" by Mary Sullivan from *101 Thematic Poems for Emergent Readers* (Scholastic, 1999). Copyright © 1999 by Mary Sullivan. Used by permission of the author.

Seeds & Plants

"I Am an Oak" by Helen H. Moore from *A Poem a Day* (Scholastic, 1997). Copyright © 1997 by Helen H. Moore. Used by permission of the author.

"Quiet Seeds" by Jodi Simpson from *Circle Time Poetry: Science* (Scholastic, 2005). Copyright © 2005 by Jodi Simpson. Used by permission of the author.

"Strawberries" and "Sunflowers" by Beth Sycamore. Copyright © 2010 by Beth Sycamore.

Seasons

"Autumn Leaves" by Jodi Simpson from *Circle Time Poetry: Around the Year* (Scholastic, 2005). Copyright © 2005 by Jodi Simpson. Used by permission of the author.

"Frost" by Kathleen M. Hollenbeck from *The Big Book of Classroom Poems* (Scholastic, 2004). Copyright © 2004 by Kathleen M. Hollenbeck. Used by permission of the author.

"Spring" by Vince Novelli. Copyright © 2010 by Vince Novelli. Used by permission of Joan Novelli for the author.

"Summer Memories" by Beth Sycamore. Copyright © 2010 by Beth Sycamore.

Earth & Sky

"Cloud Gazing" and "A Starry Zoo" by Beth Sycamore. Copyright © 2010 by Beth Sycamore.

"Goodnight, Sun" by Helen H. Moore from *Light and Shadow, I Can Read About Science Library*. Copyright © 1996 by Scholastic Inc. Used by permission of the publisher.

"Under the Ground" by Rhoda W. Bacmeister is reprinted from *Stories to Begin On* by Rhoda W. Bacmeister. Copyright © 1940 by E. P. Dutton and renewed 1968 by Rhoda W. Bacmeister.